TIGHTROPE TO TOMORROW

Tightrope to Tomorrow

PENSIONS, PRODUCTIVITY, AND
PUBLIC EDUCATION

Morton J. Marcus

With Illustrations by Dave Coverly

TECHNOS PRESS
Bloomington, Indiana

Published by TECHNOS Press of the Agency for Instructional Technology
Box A, Bloomington, IN 47402-0120
© 1997
All rights reserved

First Edition

ISBN 0-7842-0866-2
Library of Congress Catalog Card Number: 97-60407

The paper used in this publication meets the minimum requirements
of American National Standard for Information Sciences—
Permanence of Paper for Printed
Library Materials, ANSI Z39.48-1984.

Inari, *Book Design and Composition*
Dave Coverly, *Illustrator*
Karla Dunn, *Graphics Designer*
Sukanya Dutta-White, *Editor*
Mardell Raney, *Manager,* TECHNOS Press

Printed by Thomson Shore, 7300 W. Joy Road, Dexter, MI 48130-9701, USA

For
Samantha, Eric, Kaitlyn, Jeanette,
Alejandro, and Cristina —
who will carry the burden we leave
and who can share a wonderful world,
if we are thoughtful

Contents

List of Figures

ACKNOWLEDGMENTS AND REGRETS

You would not be reading this book if Mardell Raney[*] of the Agency for Instructional Technology (AIT) had not insisted on closure. I would have included more ideas and more data had she not threatened to publish with half the pages blank.

If the text is readable, Sukanya Dutta-White of AIT deserves the credit. Her passion for clarity exceeded my attachment to complexity.

Dozens of authorities on education and public finance have expressed the thoughts contained here better than I. It is not possible to credit them all. Special mention must be made of Steve Stoughton, John Augenblick, Kent McGuire, and Percy Clark, who discussed aspects of this book with me during its early stages.

Members of the staff at the Education Commission of the States and the U.S. Department of Education provided numerous leads to productive paths and warnings about intellectual cul-de-sacs. I wish I could have included more of the enormous wealth of materials these good people made available. The nation is fortunate to have such fine resources.

I regret that the data in this book are not always as up-to-date as they should be. The fault lies, not with the agencies of government that produce these data, but with the people and the Congress of the United States who fail to provide sufficient resources for statistical efforts. In several places, I deliberately used 1992 data to maintain comparability. While some data for 1995 were available when this book was written in 1996, many data series were delayed by the government shut-down of 1995, and others traditionally run two to three years late.

Roadblocks and encumbrances to progress were cleared by Rebecca Marcus, my wife, who thoughtfully helped me examine every idea and suffered every expression of despair. Additional blockages were cleared by clarifying conversations with Chuck Coffey and Larry Barnhill.

My colleagues Susan Brudvig and Carol Rogers helped assemble some

---

[*] Manager, TECHNOS Press

of the information used in these pages. DeVon Yoho, of Ball State University, made several excellent suggestions that have been inadequately incorporated.

To my colleagues in the economics profession, I extend my apologies if the inclusion of humor is seen to diminish the obscurity of expression that is requisite to dignity. Errors in analysis or interpretation contained herein are the result of my failure to subscribe to the right journals.

Finally, I am indebted to

my mother, Lena, who taught me humility—years ago, when upon hearing that I was featured on the front page of our local newspaper, she asked, "What did you do? Steal something?"

my father, Solomon, who taught me to substitute productive depression for the incapacitation of anxiety, and

my brother, Philip, who taught me to aspire to the unachievable.

All other faults to be found in this work, not deflected by these disclaimers, are the result of a fatty diet, insufficient exercise, and the stubbornness of a born-again troglodyte.

Cast of Characters

Septum Sixpack is a widower in his late 60s. He has retired from the factory just a few blocks away, where he worked for more than 40 years. These days he sits on the front porch, rocking, sipping beer, smoking inexpensive cigars, and proclaiming with conviction that most new ideas won't work.

Henna Homestead is the willowy widow across the street, who rents rooms in her large old home and putters about the garden. In Septum's eyes, Henna is Katharine Hepburn, and he is Humphrey Bogart in the *African Queen*. He sees her as unapproachable and imagines that she rejects both him and his habits. But Septum feels certain she can be won over by his tenacity and competence, if he only had the opportunity to demonstrate his virtues.

Septum and Henna both own big homes in a neighborhood of large houses, broad sidewalks, and towering shade trees. All these are relics of a time when the factory paid good wages to its workers and heavy taxes to the local government.

Serina Seriatim, Septum's seven-year-old granddaughter, is his chief link to the neighborhood. She is the neighborhood mosquito, an innocent carrier of information viruses. Although she is charming, she doesn't understand everything she hears. She loves to use information to inflame well-known passions.

Serina is a younger edition of Septum's daughter, Suzannah, whose one great crime, in Septum's eyes, was marrying an accountant, Sheldon Seriatim, referred to as "that parasitic CPA" by Septum.

Suzannah is the same age as her husband. She attended college, but is not affiliated with any political party, church, or social organization. She is intelligent, but not always confident, even though she is often passionate about her ideas and the world she lives in and does not hesitate to argue with either Sheldon or Septum. She is deeply involved in her child's upbringing, is an active PTA member, and knows exactly what she does not want in her daughter's life.

SHELDON is in his mid-30s and upwardly mobile on the socio-economic ladder. He is indifferent to affiliations of any kind, except those necessary to his career. He is not dull, but he is almost one-dimensional. His greatest passion in life is studying numbers (preferably of dollar amounts) and anything that affects them, such as education. Despite his belief in marriage as an "equal partnership," he regresses to chauvinism now and then, and leaves the raising of their child almost completely to his wife.

Serina is Septum's seven-year-old granddaughter
and the neighborhood mosquito, an innocent
carrier of information viruses.

Introduction

I am not vain enough to suppose I can suggest any new ideas upon . . . education in general. . . .

—Noah Webster

When Mike Sullivan and Carole Novak of AIT (the Agency for Instructional Technology) suggested that I write this book, Mike said, "If we wanted a scholarly work, we would have gone to a scholar." Hence, scholars should feel secure; this book offers no competition.

This is not a book for specialists about the details of education finance or education policy. Those are topics that have become too complicated for ordinary mortals to understand.

Instead, this is a book for citizens who are concerned about how America will pay for its schools and meet its obligations to its senior citizens in the years ahead. The two matters are connected. I offer a set of observations and recommendations for financing education in America, based on a larger view of contemporary issues.

Some readers will dismiss my ideas as "off-the-wall." Others will reject my views because they are against the tide of political sentiment in America today. A few persons may concur with my conclusions, yet find them too idealistic to be politically acceptable. That is not a serious concern. Idealism is a virtue, to be counted as an asset both for the individual and in the social accounts of the nation. If these pages stimulate discussions of education finance and other matters of public policy, my objectives will have been met.

Where are we?

As America enters the 21st century, several progressive aspects of the 20th century are being reexamined and modified. Contrary to liberal cant, this is not a reactionary renaissance. Nor are we rejecting oppressive liberal programs that conservatives have despised and feared for so many years. We are just following an American tradition of pragmatic revisionism. Nonetheless, we are confused, as we have been for more than two centuries, by our strongly held, but opposing, beliefs.

America is philosophically schizophrenic. We are simultaneously Jeffersonian and Hamiltonian on most issues. We believe in both the virtues of the small enterprise and the effectiveness of concerted, centralized authority. We view mankind as both noble and sinful. Slight changes in public sentiment cause the seesaw of politics to tilt from one position to the other with rapidity and ease.

The values and hopes for political and economic achievement that arose in the 18th century and matured in the 19th were advancing nicely until the mid-1970s. They were accelerated by the hardships of the Great Depression, the revived idealism of World War II, and the economic advances of the postwar era. Then, Vietnam, Watergate, and economic trauma (industrial restructuring, job losses, and inflation) in the 1970s began to erode support for progress through collective action. Gender gaps and separations by age groups became as important as race and economic class in dividing Americans. Atomistic views, stressing individualism, regained popularity. A new technology, the personal computer, reinforced concepts of a society built on independence rather than interdependence.

Now, in the late-1990s, America is in full retreat from the Great Society. The dreams that were slowly being transformed into reality are being denigrated as unreasonable expectations. And we are searching for new approaches to persistent problems.

It is in this context that America continues to debate education issues. As in years past, we expect education to solve our major social and economic problems. At the same time, we blame our schools and our educators for a host of social and economic problems. In addition, we are justifiably uncomfortable with how we finance our local schools. We are increasingly separated from their operation and governance. We publish an endless stream of documents, reports, books, and manifestos, highlighting, but not correcting, their faults.

Where is this book going?

It is not too dramatic to say that America is about to walk a tightrope. We have ahead of us a distinctive challenge. Our goal, the safe landing at the end of that taut wire, is a healthy and secure old age for millions of Americans. How can we get there? The wire—the path—we must follow is education. We approach that wire in chapter 1 with two unanswerable questions: Are we spending too much on education? and, What do we want from education?

The answer to these unanswerable questions may depend on how well we understand the problems created by an aging population and the distant platform we hope to reach. Thus, in chapter 2, we consider the aging of America and the implications of this great demographic force for our economy and our education system. Chapter 3 looks more closely at the role of education in the American economy.

Changes in our expectations about the contributions of education to the economy may necessitate changes in the organization of education. This topic is explored in chapter 4, while chapter 5 looks at the financial poles holding the education highwire in place. Beyond how we currently pay for education are the questions of who should pay for education (chapter 6) and who should run the schools (chapter 7).

Finally, before we venture out on to that wire, before we take the path that leads to the other side of the chasm, chapter 8 looks at the issue of choice, which could replace or seriously fray the tightrope we have been using for more than a century, the public school.

From time to time, various characters appear in these pages. In case you wonder, they are fictional and only resemble your neighbors and relatives. They are here to augment the arguments and provide relief from the discourse. Sometimes they are embedded in the text, and at other times they appear in separate boxes, to which you may switch as you would change channels with your TV clicker.

———

"It won't work, you know," Septum Sixpack said, rocking with conviction. "You can't go around restructuring the way we finance our schools and changing the balance between the various levels of government. Folks just won't have it."

(continued)

We were sitting on the front porch of Septum's home, which he used as an observatory — to watch Henna Homestead, the widow who rented rooms and puttered about the garden across the way. "Can't do it," he continued. "Too many hurdles, too much doubt, too much trying to change the way folks think about schools. Gets right to the core of local control. And it won't work."

"What," I said, "are we talking about?" "Fool book you've written," he said, surveying the giant rhododendron bushes in the Homestead front yard for signs of Henna's presence.

"How do you know what I've written?" I asked. "Everybody knows your book. You've used it for months as an excuse to avoid everything you don't want to do," Septum sneered.

"But you don't know what's in the book," I insisted. "Don't need to read it," he replied. "I know everything in your head from talking to Serina. She goes over there, and you talk to her, and then she comes back over here and talks to me. Don't take no special training by the CIA to know you're pushing higher taxes, advocating federal control of the schools, and wanting to cut local school boards down to nothing at all."

Serina Seriatim is Septum's granddaughter, a frequent visitor to our house. She is the neighborhood mosquito, an innocent carrier of information viruses.

"Hold on," I said, "your granddaughter doesn't necessarily understand everything she hears. And, you know as well as I, she loves to use information to inflame well-known passions. She is your daughter's daughter." "You leave Suzannah out of this," Septum blazed, defending his daughter, whose one great crime, in his eyes, was marrying an accountant. "Suzannah, my darling Serina, and that parasitic CPA Sheldon are the only family I have left," he sighed, as his eyes scanned the garden across the street.

"Exactly," I declared, "you and millions of others who are retired or are going to be retired soon. All you have is Suzannah, Sheldon, and Serina. Broadly speaking, that's all any of us have. Those retirees are coming from the great baby boom of the 40s, 50s, and early 60s. But most people just do not appreciate its significance. That's what I was trying to tell Serina one day when she was watching me write. The greatest force in America for the last half of the 20th century and the first third of the next is the baby boom." "And the baby boomers put all the pressure on the schools in the past?" Septum asked in a hollow voice, as he spotted Henna.

"Right," I continued, even though I knew that I had only his ear and not his brain. "Since the 1960s, those baby boomers have been changing markets and redirecting resources. Soon they'll have their impact on social security and pension programs." "So what?" he asked, now turning his rocker to face directly toward the presumed Garden of Eden just beyond the flow of traffic. "So what?" I echoed. "So we now have to provide for the health care and retirement income of approximately 70 million Americans." "Do not," he said, smoothing down his few rumpled locks of hair. "Folks like me have their retirement income and social security. I did it all myself. I saved and put money aside in the stock market, and I have my pension. I don't depend on anybody. Don't need to have nobody's help on that." "Do, too," I countered, ignoring the invalidating double negative. "Who's going to pay the taxes to support your monthly social security checks? Who's going to create the profits that will pay the dividends which give your stocks value? Every person expecting to live without earning income in the years ahead will be dependent on the income generated by those at work. And how do we get higher levels of income?"

Septum was not listening. Henna was on her toes, her arms extended to trim some overhanging limbs. The display had caused Septum's auditory receptors to yield entirely to his visual input mechanism.

"Well, I'll tell you," I persisted. "This country has to generate earnings by having an internationally competitive labor force. And that is Suzannah and Sheldon today, joined by Serina in a few years. You don't want to be denied your retirement pleasures, to take less income. You don't want to be forced into seeking employment because your social security check is inadequate and your pension insufficient. That's why you should support measures to help today's and tomorrow's workers become more capable of generating income.

"And how do we do that?" I knew I was talking to myself, but I went on. "We reopen our school systems to our former students. We use our school resources to go into the community, the offices, factories, and homes of adults who are 25 to 45 years old today, and we help them learn what they did not learn when they were in school.

"And how do we pay for that, Septum? Do you want to see the federal deficit grow? Do you want this country to go further into debt?" "NO!" he roared. There's nothing like debt and deficit to get Septum's attention. "Blasted government is going to drag us all to perdition." He was listening again, on guard, attentive. "Right," I agreed. "We need to spend money carefully, and we need to pay for the things we *want. That's fiscal responsibility. That's the mature conduct of government affairs."*

"Hmm," he grunted in concurrence.

"So," I proceeded, "we need to raise taxes. In addition, there are funds currently used to hide the extent of the federal deficit. These we could use to assure every Serina, wherever she may live, a good, fundamental base of financial support for her education from kindergarten through high school."

"And that's how you're going to do it, isn't it?" he smirked triumphantly. "You're going to raise taxes and have the federal government dole out money with heavy chains attached. You'll lure schools into the control of the Department of Education with the carrot of federal funds, and then slam them with mandated programs. You'll have Big Brother telling schools all over America what they should teach, and how they should teach it." "Did you hear me say that?" I protested. "You don't have to say it," Septum responded, his eyes flashing with anger. "Just let the Feds get their funding foot in the door, and there will be regulations and mandates coming out of every window before long."

I told him my ideas to defuse the situation. "Those are easy things to say," Septum replied pensively, as his eyes drifted to Henna hauling a garden hose into position for an arboreal libation.

"And difficult to do? Yes," I agreed. "But we don't have the luxury of arguing for a decade. Those baby boomers will be demanding more and more health care in the next few years, and they will want their full retirement income shortly thereafter. America needs to expand income. We don't want you and Suzannah, and ultimately Serina, contesting over a small pie. Improving education is one way of increasing the size of the pie we all must share."

"You're right," Septum said, rising from his rocking chair. "A nice piece of pie would be good. Maybe you could go over and ask what's-her-name there if she'd like to join us. I'll go cut a few slices of apple pie or whatever's in the kitchen and make a pot of coffee."

"Sure," I responded, "what's-her-name and whatever. Sounds good to me. Be right back."[1]

Tightrope to Tomorrow

TIGHTROPE TO TOMORROW

Only the rising moon or the appearance of
Henna could make him stop.

One

Perspectives on Education

> . . . *criticism of the public schools spread throughout the country.*
> *Critics attacked the results of public education, its bureaucratic*
> *structure, and especially . . . its costs.*
>
> — Michael B. Katz

The time was the 1870s, but the issues remain the same today. Perceived costs, the perennial problem, are too high. Perceived benefits are inadequate. The entire system is suspect.

Debates about education center on two persistent questions:

1. Are we spending too much?

and

2. What do we want from education?

These questions are related. How can we tell if we are spending too much if we do not know what we expect education to produce? Traditionally, we try to weigh the costs of an activity against its benefits. If we have little idea of the benefits we desire or the benefits actually received, we are inhibited from judging whether we are spending too much or too little. In addition, if we have only a vague concept of how those benefits would change with variations in spending, we cannot make precise decisions about the right level of expenditure.

In our daily lives, we do these things implicitly and become overwrought if we attempt precise calculations. When my friend and neighbor, Septum Sixpack, buys beer for the weekend, he knows, based on experience, how much beer he and his friends will require to achieve the desired state of inebriation. He calculates, without thinking about it, the benefits of additional quantities against the expenditure required.

But when Septum goes to buy a new automobile, he becomes confused if he has to consider all the factors of choice: miles per gallon, styling, electronic options, and seat coverings. If you tell him that the purchase price is only part of the total cost of an automobile, he will not invite you to his Super Bowl party. He does not want to hear that insurance, maintenance, gasoline consumption, and tire wear should be included in his calculations. In addition, Septum will have a fist for your nose if you persist in detailing the costs each model imposes on society through pollution, traffic congestion, and the utilization of parking space.

Education is not like beer or a car. Consumer goods are generally for private use by the person who makes the purchase. Septum does not see himself "buying" education. He pays for it with taxes imposed by the state and the local school authority. The education he buys is not for himself but for his children and/or the children of other people.

The benefits of education are not like those of beer. The very first gulp of beer is often delightfully refreshing, and further consumption offers, after just a brief delay, a nice buzz. Education may not show any perceptible benefits for years. Then, the benefits may accrue to individuals other than those who receive the schooling. Co-workers, other family members, society in general can benefit from the education of any given person.

"No way I'll sign your darn petition," Septum told his daughter. "But, Father," Suzannah pleaded, "we want to get a new school built here. That decrepit dungeon where Serina goes . . ."

"Hold it right there," Septum interrupted. "That school was here when your mother and I moved in here, and it was plenty good enough for you. It's even got air conditioning and stuff nobody ever needed to get a decent education when I went to school. All you're going to do is raise property taxes and bring down the prices on our houses."

"Not so," Suzannah responded. "Sheldon says property values will rise if we have a good school that can provide modern facilities for today's education needs."

"Sheldon, your creepy CPA says," he mimicked her. "CPA! Must stand for Couldn't Prove Anything. I won't sign and that's that."

Septum Sixpack does not make many choices in his purchase of education. When he buys beer, he makes his choice based on a few factors—taste, image, and price. But the quality and nature of the education his taxes support are determined by where he chooses to live. That choice is complicated by all the other attributes of housing, of which education is but one consideration.

Septum does not choose a housing locale because of its school district, unless he has school-age children in his home. He is not directly involved in curriculum decisions, in hiring practices, or in the multitude of issues that constitute education in America today. But Septum probably has strong opinions on all these factors.

In buying beer, Septum Sixpack does not get involved in the production process, does not set hiring policies, is not concerned with either worker discipline or the morals of the company's directors. If he is concerned about such matters, he can easily switch from one brand to another because there are numerous substitutes offered in the market.

Septum's housing choice determines the school district he must support through the coercive powers of taxation. He can opt to move. He can send his children to a private school or can educate them at home. But he must support the public schools. He does not have to support Budweiser if he is offended by their advertisements or their environmental policies. He must support the schools whether he agrees or disagrees with their practices and policies.

Serina was helping Henna Homestead weed the flowers in the side yard. "How do you like school?" she asked the little girl. "It's OK," the seed of the Seriatims answered. "But why do I have to go to school?"

"For the same reason you are pulling up those weeds," Henna replied. "If the flowers are to be healthy, they cannot be strangled by plants which do not contribute to the well-being of the garden. School is where young girls and boys learn how to become flowers, to contribute to the beauty and well-being of the garden. Otherwise, they will grow up as troublesome weeds."

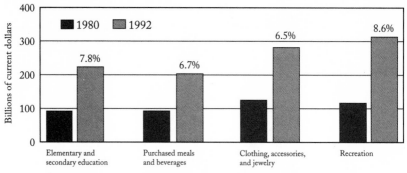

(Numbers above the bars are average annual percent increases from 1980 to 1992)

Figure 1.1 Comparative Expenditures

Are we spending too much on education?

How can we put state and local government spending for education in perspective? Consider these facts. Consumers spent $318 billion on recreation in 1992 while state and local governments spent $229 billion on primary and secondary education. (See *Figure 1.1.*) Recreation expenditures averaged an 8.6% increase in the preceding 12 years compared to a 7.8% growth for education. We spent 72 cents on education for every dollar we spent on recreation in 1992. Alternatively, we spent $1.23 on clothing, accessories, and jewelry for each dollar spent on education.

Public spending for elementary and secondary education in 1980 was $93 billion dollars. That same year, Americans also spent $93 billion on meals and beverages eaten away from home. In the intervening years, as everyone knows, eating out has boomed. It grew annually by 6.7% on average between 1980 and 1992. But we might be surprised to know that all consumer expenditures grew even faster, at a 7.4% average annual rate. Nonetheless, during that same period, state and local expenditures for primary and secondary education advanced still faster, at a 7.8% rate.[1] If eating out is booming, then what explosive sound is education making?

Politicians and taxpayers alike will say that primary and secondary education absorbs an increasing portion of state and local government expenditures. This is contrary to fact: education equaled 25.3% of state

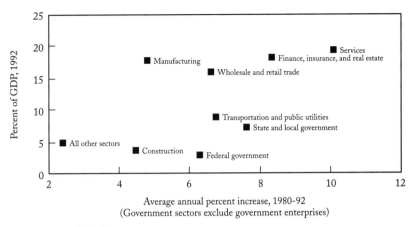

Figure 1.2 The Economy
Not adjusted for inflation, GDP grew by 6.9% from 1980 to 1992

and local government expenditures in 1980 and decreased to 23.6% in 1992. But facts are only obstructions in the road of rant and rhetoric.

The problem that voters and government officials perceive correctly is that state and local governments account for an increased share of the nation's output. From 1980 to 1992, as the federal government's purchases of goods and services became a smaller portion of our nation's economy (down from 3.5% to 3.3%), the state and local government sector increased (from 7.2% to 7.7%). We can accept the blessings of reduced defense expenditures and applaud the reduced role of the federal government. But there is no escaping the fact that purchases of goods and services by all levels of government (excluding government enterprises) rose (however slightly) from 10.7% of Gross Domestic Product (GDP) in 1980 to 11% in 1992. Within the American economy, state and local government has been the third fastest growing sector. (See *Figure 1.2*.)

This has been a transition from missiles against communism to missions of compassion. But it does not reduce anti-government fervor. Since the role of government is to protect and defend (see chapter 4), money spent on armaments is easily understood and appreciated. But many Americans are not prepared to meet social needs through the auspices of government.

Although elementary and secondary education has been the largest single element (23.6%) of state and local government expenditures, it has

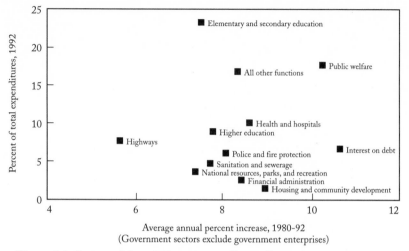

Figure 1.3 State and Local Government Expenditures

Not adjusted for inflation, these grew by 8.4% from 1980 to 1992

not been the fastest growing public function. Between 1980 and 1992, the pressure on state and local government finances came not from education but from other sources. *Figure 1.3* reveals that both health and hospitals (+8.8%) and public welfare (+10.7%) grew faster than elementary and secondary education (+7.8%). These two sectors combined accounted for 25% of total expenditures during that period.

States and localities are expected (often mandated by the federal government) to care for the elderly, the indigent, and the ill (who are often the same population). In addition, an 11.6% increase in interest on the debt of these governments (from 1980 to 1992) has been the result of high interest rates and increased use of borrowing to meet short- and long-term needs. The federal government provides funding for many of its mandated welfare and health programs. But it offers little assistance for education.

How much should be spent on education? How rapidly should those expenditures grow? We can ask the same questions of all categories of expenditure. How much should consumers spend on housing? on transportation? on medical care? *Figure 1.4* shows that from 1980 to 1992, these were the three leading categories of consumer spending. Expendi-

TIGHTROPE TO TOMORROW

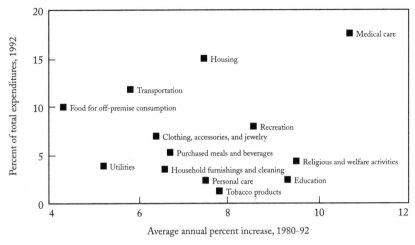

Figure 1.4 Personal Consumption Expenditures
Not adjusted for inflation, these grew by 7.4% from 1980 to 1992

tures made by households directly for education (mainly, higher education) were exceeded only by spending on tobacco products and personal care items.

No one knows how much should be spent on education. But we might properly question whether the nation would gain more if the next dollar spent were allocated to our schools rather than to our pleasures or our vanities.

What do we want from education?

Public education has been seen as a means of changing society since the days of Horace Mann and the education reformers of the 19th century. We have loaded many of our attempts to improve society into the lunch pails of young people and sent them off to school where, it was presumed, they would learn to resolve all the issues we either could not or would not. *Figure 1.5* may well represent the complex structure of the modern school in America.

If the labor supply is not what we wish it to be, then it is the responsibility of the schools to prepare students for the world of work. Deficien-

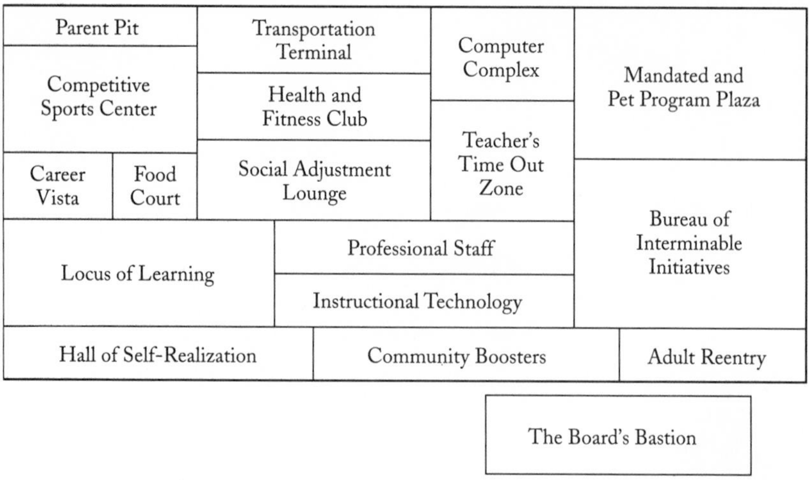

Parent Pit

Transportation Terminal

Computer Complex

Mandated and Pet Program Plaza

Competitive Sports Center

Health and Fitness Club

Teacher's Time Out Zone

Career Vista

Food Court

Social Adjustment Lounge

Bureau of Interminable Initiatives

Locus of Learning

Professional Staff

Instructional Technology

Hall of Self-Realization

Community Boosters

Adult Reentry

The Board's Bastion

Figure 1.5 The Modern School

cies in punctuality or high rates of absenteeism at the factory or office are not addressed in the workplace. Business leaders expect the schools to do the job, to inculcate appropriate values that improve productivity.

If racial discord is a problem, if segregation exists in local housing markets, we require the schools to implement bussing plans to achieve among the children what the adults will not accept for themselves. The monetary and social costs of bussing for racial integration are presumed to be less than those of addressing the problem where it originates, in the behavior of individuals making residential location choices.

If parents do not sustain an environment at home that prepares young people for school, then we have no choice but to extend the reach of the schools to younger and younger students. Head Start will overcome the home environment. We would not, however, think of imposing upon the parents themselves!

If communities seek entertainment and identity, then the schools should build athletic facilities to feed the extra-curricular needs of the town. Many Americans will support any effort that involves dressing young people in costumes. Perhaps we could bring back Latin to the classroom by forming teams where the participants wore togas and the losers were fed to the lions.

If school administrators behave in an arbitrary fashion and teachers respond by forming unions, we wring our hands and denounce the labor movement. Each year, we spend hundreds of millions of dollars on teacher training and, more recently, on teacher assessment, but we have virtually no training for school board members and little effective performance evaluation of school administrators. And we have yet to learn how to work with teachers, in or out of unions, on substantive progress for education.

If the structure of employment is changing, if firms are downsizing, we do not ask how employees could be used by those firms in more productive ways. Instead, we declare that schools should prepare the workers of the future for flexible careers.

If real estate developers keep building new homes further and further from our central cities, we extend our bus services to the new residential areas and, ultimately, build new schools in those suburban areas. At the same time, we seek imaginative alternative uses for abandoned city schools.

If we anticipated an invasion from Mars, no doubt there would be an outcry for teaching the Martian language and culture in our schools. America's schools are expected to be the passive, residual answer to social and economic problems. Schools are expected to accommodate change, regardless of the costs it imposes.

This phenomenon is not truly unusual. In former times, the church was believed to have mystical powers. Mythical kings could pull swords from boulders. In our times, schools are thought capable

"You should sign this petition," Sheldon instructed his father-in-law. "Won't," was the answer, as Septum sipped from a bottle of beer he had opened several hours earlier.

"Education is the route to increased productivity," Sheldon explained, refusing to give up. "Might be." Septum was unenthusiastic. "Might be hard work and not fancy foolery that's needed," he added. "Might be the kids should take jobs and pay for better schools themselves, rather than working to put louder boom boxes in their egos-on-wheels. Schools should teach character, and productivity will follow. We used to have a character code on the wall at my school . . ." Sheldon prepared to leave. Whenever Septum started on "the character code," only the rising moon or the appearance of Henna across the way could make him stop.

of resolving all problems. Although teachers and administrators complain about the lack of respect they enjoy in society, their mythical position is unchallenged.

In many cases, the use of schools as scapegoats in public debates is a delaying action to forestall dealing with today's difficulties. Sometimes, however, our schools may be the most efficient means to solving problems. Other social institutions are not geared to long-term efforts. Employers or not-for-profit agencies might attempt to resolve complex problems in the short term because they must show results quickly. This may prove more costly than leaving the resolution of issues to the magic of inter-generational transformations in which the schools excel.

Yet, the problem before America today—not lying ahead, but here with us now—may go well beyond our children. Today, the task for our schools may be to reclaim the abandoned and neglected generation now in the labor force. In addition to preparing young people to be effective members of society, our schools may be called upon to use their resources and talents to educate adults who are not prepared to meet their adult responsibilities.

This redirection of education systems arises from the specific challenges facing America as it enters the 21st century. Let us now turn to that problem and its consequences for our nation.

American retirees, of the present and future, will be able to live well if American workers have the creativity, imagination, initiative, and opportunity to generate high earnings.

Two

The Aging of America and the Demand for Education

It was Wang Lung's marriage day. . . . This was the last morning he would have to light the fire. . . . And if the woman wearied, there would be her children to light the fire, the many children she would bear to Wang Lung. [He] thought of children running in and out of their three rooms. Three rooms had always seemed much to them, a house half empty since his mother died. . . .

"Now, how can two lone men need so much room? Cannot father and son sleep together? The warmth of the young one's body will comfort the old one's cough."

But the father always replied, "I am saving my bed for my grandson. He will warm my bones in my age."

—Pearl S. Buck

In *The Good Earth*, Pearl Buck was writing of China before the revolutions of the 20th century. In those days, a young man stayed in his father's house. In time, however, the father would be living in the house of his child. Successive generations provided sustenance for those who gave them life, and children and grandchildren were expected to comfort the elderly. The father had a traditional claim on the income of his son, who, in turn, thought of the claims he would have on the labor of his wife and the children she would bear.

The words of Pearl Buck would have been less applicable to Americans. Our character, our institutions, and our expectations were formed by successive waves of immigrants coming to these shores.[1] Whether those immigrants came here for religious freedom or economic opportunity, their departure from the old country normally involved severing or loosening family ties. We have never been, despite our Norman Rockwell mythology, a nation of strong family relations, comparable to China.

Americans were people who left Mama and Papa somewhere in the east, if not in the old country. The settlers, who moved from the Tidewater to the Piedmont, through the mountains to the Great Plains, and ultimately to Hollywood, were willing to pack up and move out. In time, they would remember Mama with a card and/or a phone call on Mother's Day. The plays *I Remember Mamma* and *Life with Father* became hits to compensate for the reality of deserting the family fireside.

Unsentimental Americans were undeterred by family considerations in the pursuit of their Manifest Destiny. They did not stay close to home or even bring the old folks along when they migrated west. (An exception: Steinbeck's Joad family moved intact because they had lost the farm.) Most Americans on the move left the old homestead because they did not believe it could support them as well as the new lands to the west.

Contemporary claims on income

Today, we raise our children to be self-supporting. We seem to believe that each generation must assume responsibility for its own welfare. Parents will support their children until the young have acquired the skills needed to enter the job market or have achieved an age suitable for separation from the family. Sometimes, we just throw the kids out, or they leave when intergenerational stress becomes too much. This is possible where economic opportunities are abundant. Americans can afford the luxury of keeping parents and children in separate households.

Modern parents do not welcome their offspring's return to the nest. When Martin Luther King, Jr., looked forward to the day when African-Americans could say "Free at last, free at last, Great God Almighty, we're free at last," it had a different significance from today. Now, these words are the delighted cry of parents as they see their children leave the homestead.

But our generations are not independent of one another. Our elders still have claims on the economic efforts of their children. The change we have introduced in the 20th century is that we are now dependent on our neighbors' children, rather than solely upon our own. Today, pensions, social security, medicare, and medicaid are the claims made by older citizens upon the income of the young. Those claims are exercised through dividends and taxes paid by profitable companies, plus the taxes based on the income of younger people. In traditional society of the old world, the father had a claim on the sweat and toil of his child. You and I possess claims on the income generated by the children of other people. We exercise those claims through our tax system and the market mechanism.

Although some Americans still believe that social security is or should be a simple fiduciary relationship between individuals and the government, it is not. Each worker has an "account" with the government, representing taxes collected during that person's working years. A fiduciary program would involve investment of the money in those accounts such that the accumulated premiums, plus earned income through dividends and interest, and perhaps capital appreciation, would provide the basis for periodic payments upon retirement. But the monthly checks retirees receive today from the social security administration are far in excess of what they would draw if only their "accounts" with the federal trust fund were the basis for payment.

Older Americans on social security are paid from taxes levied on workers and their employers.[2] The trust fund is "invested" in U.S. government securities. Monthly payments into those "accounts" are lent to the federal government to finance our nation's deficit spending. The rate of return is meager, and there is no capital appreciation as there might be if the funds were invested in traditional equity markets. Today's payments are a function of decisions by the Congress, rather than the result of a planned investment program.

Medicare, payments to health care providers (not to older citizens) for services to persons 65 and older, is also financed by taxes and administered in a comparable trust fund. Medicaid, payments to health care providers (not to older citizens) for services to the poor (many of whom are elderly), operates without any trust fund fiction.[3] It is financed by the federal and state governments through their current general revenues—taxes on individuals and corporations.

Each of these three programs gives America's senior citizens claims on the income generated by businesses. If our taxes were lower, wages and/or dividends to owners could be higher. Alternatively, prices paid by consumers could be lower. But federal taxes take some of the income produced by labor and capital, as well as income realized by selling products or services to consumers. Then, the government provides either transfers to the elderly (social security checks) or payments for services to the elderly (medicare and medicaid).

Private pensions are also claims on the income generated by businesses. Most pension funds are invested in the stock market. Workers or their employers put money into retirement accounts or mutual funds. Typically, that money is then used to buy stocks or bonds of corporations. The stocks pay dividends out of the earnings of the corporation. Bonds also pay interest out of those earnings. Again, workers, stockholders, or consumers could be rewarded by higher salaries, higher dividends, or lower prices if the corporation did not have these claims on its income.

Retired people do not think of themselves as having claims on the income of others. The father in Pearl Buck's story had explicit and obvious claims. He got his food, shelter, and clothing as a result of his son's labor. If he owned the land his son farmed, then the father had a claim on the income of the farm, as its owner. But that income could not be produced without someone's labor.

Most Americans see their retirement income as their due. Federal government payments are justified by the fact that "we won the War and made this country great." It does not matter which war. Participation in the generation that fought is considered sufficient to grant the retiree a claim on income. It is as if each citizen, at the conclusion of the war, was given an equity interest in the national corporation. That monthly social security check and those medicare or medicaid payments are the just dividends due the defenders of the nation.

Holders of private pensions, by possessing stocks through their retirement funds, are owners of American businesses.[4] They have established legal rights to the earnings of the corporation. The extent to which stock holders are able to enjoy healthy dividends depends on the earnings of the corporation. And those earnings are a function of the competitive position of the company. More and more, corporate competitiveness is a function of the quality of its labor and management. When we buy stock, we buy not only the accumulated capital of a corporation but also the skills of its employees and the talents of its management to use such skills well.

Claims on income through taxation are also dependent on how well people apply their accumulated knowledge. Ultimately, the government can tax individuals and corporations only to the extent that they generate income. The more income earned, the greater the taxes paid to the government. Higher tax receipts then enhance the government's ability to pay the claims of the elderly.

To the extent that human capital is formed in schools, or is assisted in its formation by schools, the education of our neighbors' children becomes a determinant of the income we can expect upon retirement. In his later years, Pearl Buck's farmer can live only as well as permitted by his children's capability to generate products or services, whether or not they are exchanged in the marketplace. In addition, his well-being depends on their willingness to honor his claims on their income.

So, too, American retirees, of the present and future, will be able to live well if American workers have the creativity, imagination, initiative, and opportunity to generate high earnings. In addition, those workers, their corporations, and government must be willing to honor the claims on income held by older citizens.

The baby boom reconsidered

Some things are so obvious that we ignore them. That which is familiar is often unseen, as we scan the heavens for omens. One of the most obvious characteristics of America is the age distribution of its population. We have all heard so much about the baby boom and its implications for society that we can go about our daily activities without giving it another thought.

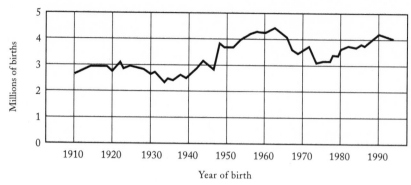

Figure 2.1 U.S. Births, 1909 to 1993

Yet, the continuing debate in Congress over the budget deficit is driven by the most obvious fact: America will have a rapidly increasing number of older citizens in the future. These citizens will have significant claims, through the public or private sector, on the income produced by our economy. That income must be produced by our neighbors' children, and those claims must be honored, or we risk unprecedented social conflict.

Increasing the capabilities of American workers to produce income should be Congress' leading objective. However, many citizens and their representatives believe that the day of reckoning, when the vast number of seniors begin to exercise their claims, is far away. They ignore the fact that it takes a considerable period of time either to develop new human capital or to improve the existing one. They also do not understand that our economic Armageddon is closer than they think.

Most people subscribe to the view that the baby boom began in 1946. That year, after the discharge of millions of Americans from military service, births did soar. After declining in 1944 and 1945, births in the U.S. exceeded 3.4 million in 1946 and topped 3.8 million in 1947. (See *Figure 2.1.*) These were monumental annual increases. In 1946, births grew by 553,000 (+19.3%) and an additional 405,000 (+11.9%) in 1947.

Then, in the 1950s and early 1960s, American women, presumably in conjunction with American men, brought forth babies with as much zest as our factories producing autos, washing machines, and television sets.

Tightrope to Tomorrow

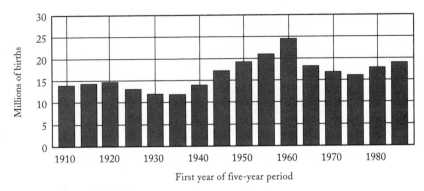

Figure 2.2 U.S. Births
By five-year periods

Has any other nation ever had such an increase in fecundity? This was more than just compensation for the delay in family development brought on by World War II and the Depression that preceded it. This was an unexplained phenomenon that has kept demographers and economists generating hypotheses for more than 40 years.

The traditional view that the baby boom began in 1946 may be questioned when the data are examined closely. Reconsider *Figure 2.1*. It is clearly evident that the decline in births bottomed out at the low point of the Great Depression in 1933. The next few years saw a slight, erratic increase in births. Then, in 1940, U.S. births began four years of steady, significant increase. If we reorganize the data into five-year periods, as in *Figure 2.2*, we can see that births grew continuously from 1940–44 until 1960–64.

These data can be made even more explicit. *Figure 2.3* shows three five-year periods during which births declined, followed by five such periods in which they increased. The increase for 1940–44 was 18.1%, second only to the great surge which followed in 1945–49 (21.5%). These percentage increases are the shocks to the demographic scene from which great changes occur with far reaching consequences.

The issue here is not why this happened, but what it will mean for America in the future. But first we must understand the simple facts and how markets and politics respond to change.

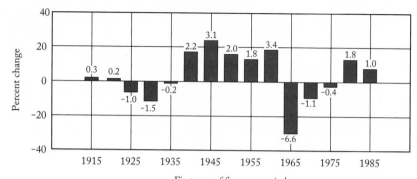

First year of five-year period
(Number shown with each bar is the change in births [in millions]
for each five-year period from the preceding five-year period)

Figure 2.3 Percent Change in U.S. Births
By five-year periods

The demographic surge

Markets and popular movements tend to follow major changes. Statistically, a major change is one which has both a significant increase or decrease in both percentage and absolute terms. When marketing decisions are made, analysts look for those places or populations that are growing and where the numbers of persons are not trivial. If a small town grows from 200 to 400 persons, the doubling of that population does not attract much attention. Large percentage increases in small numbers are not impressive. But a major percentage increase associated with big numbers does draw commercial attention. Thus, when a city of one million posts a sizable percentage increase, it will see new entrants into the market and renewed vigor from existing competitors.

The population growth which began in the early 1940s put large numbers of children into our homes. When World War II ended, these children contributed to the surge in housing demand, which characterized the immediate postwar era. By 1945–46, the edge of this wedge was entering our schools. The cumulative effect became evident as the decade closed. Old schools, in old locations, were inadequate for the new era. Temporary structures were put in place, to be followed by major school construction campaigns across the nation.

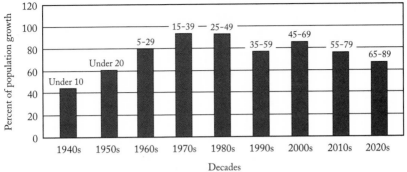

Figure 2.4 Persons Born 1940 to 1964
As a percent of U.S. population growth

Those born in the early 1940s consistently pushed whatever social or economic system they were entering. The extent of their impact depended on how prepared society was to receive them. For example, they met excess capacity in the schools. The first boomers could be accommodated in classrooms built 20 to 40 years earlier, classrooms that seemed somewhat empty for the babies of the period from 1925 to 1939. Full awareness of this surge, a sense of crisis, occurred when the second group (born from 1945 to 1949) were in the system as well.

Possibly, no force in our society has caused as much social and economic change as the surge in births that began in 1940. The great prosperity of the 1950s, at the end of the Korean War, started when the edge of this wedge was 15 years old. Wages of Americans, and the subsequent increase in buying power, were bolstered by our virtual monopoly on high-tech production and intense competition for the few new workers entering the labor market in the early 50s. Then we found our stride as the baby boomers became consumers and producers in the late 50s and early 60s. America's great period of economic expansion in the 1960s corresponded with massive increases in the number of workers available to businesses, starting about 1957.

How important have those born between 1940 and 1964 (the end of the baby boom) been to American society? In *Figure 2.4*, we see that this group accounted for 44.5% of the nation's population increase in the

1940s. In the 1970s, this cohort was 15 to 39 years of age and represented 94% of the country's population growth. Their share of population growth was about the same in the 1980s, when they were 25 to 49 years old. Even when they are 65 to 89 years old, in the 2020s, they will account for 67% of the population increase in the U.S.

Implications for the future

Pearl Buck does not tell us when the father in her story retired from the labor force. It was probably a gradual transition. In America, retirement has been a defined event centered on age 65. Persons born in 1940 will become 65 in 2005 . . . less than 10 years from now.

Thus, the implications of the baby boom for retirement and health care financing are upon us today. Those born in 1940 are now over 55, an age at which, medical statistics tell us, utilization of the health care system is already rising sharply.

This same group has become net savers. They have completed the years of family development. They have probably moved into the largest home they will ever own. Their stock of household goods also has peaked, although they are still engaged in upgrading and replacement purchases. Their thoughts are turning to increasing the amount of current income put aside for retirement. This increased flow of savings puts downward pressure on interest rates and upward pressure on stock market prices. From now until 2029, when the last of the boomers turns 65, these trends will draw increased attention.

Who will warm the bones of this generation born between 1940 and 1964? As they retire, they will seek to sustain their achieved levels of consumption and comfort. They will guard their retirement funds carefully. They will become increasingly active in defending their claims to the income produced by younger workers.

The potential for political and market pressures from this group is significant. One can imagine increased pressures for sustaining or improving the federal transfer (social security) and service (medicare and medicaid) programs now in place. Current congressional efforts to limit these

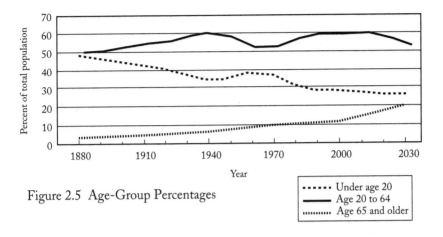

Figure 2.5 Age-Group Percentages

····· Under age 20
——— Age 20 to 64
········· Age 65 and older

programs are being taken before the boomers reach the age when they are fully attentive to their future circumstances. This may be the last opportunity for such limitations to be put in place.

The baby boomers may also seek to protect their private pensions and the dividends they expect from the private sector. Corporate dividend policies may come under more scrutiny. Current minor efforts to have businesses limit their retained earnings may be advanced. Initiatives may become more serious to have dividends equal some prescribed portion of after-tax earnings. Some boomers may push to have all such earnings returned to stockholders so that they can decide what portion they wish to reinvest in the company and what portion they wish to keep for their own current purposes.

These are issues involving the distribution of income. Of greater importance, however, to this generation and the nation at large is the task of developing the economy and the capabilities of the work force to maintain a high level of income. The claims on taxes and corporate income can only be meaningful if the economy is healthy. Otherwise, Americans will be battling over slices of a smaller pie.

Broadly speaking, income is generated by persons 20 to 64 years old. This group has been between 50% and 60% of the U.S. population since 1890. As seen in *Figure 2.5*, other age groups have been changing in their relative shares of the nation's population. In 1880, young Americans, those under age 20, were 48% of our people. That share has been declining. In

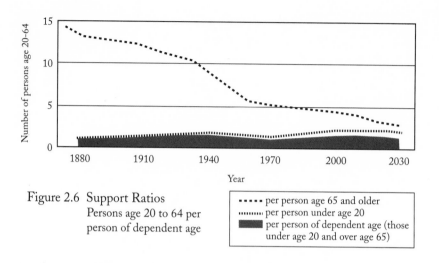

Figure 2.6 Support Ratios
Persons age 20 to 64 per
person of dependent age

- - - per person age 65 and older
.... per person under age 20
■ per person of dependent age (those under age 20 and over age 65)

1990, it was below 30%, and in 2030, it is projected to be just above 25% by the U.S. Bureau of the Census. At the same time, the population of those 65 and older has grown from just 3% in 1880 to 12.6% in 1990, and should reach 20% by 2030.

Tomorrow's adults (20 to 64 years of age) will have to support the income claims of an increasing number of people. In 1880, there was one adult for every young person (under age 20) in the country. That figure has grown moderately. (See *Figure 2.6*.) By 2030, we expect there will be two adults per young person. This increase is consistent with our observations of fewer children per family.

At the same time, we have seen a dramatic decrease in the number of adults per citizen age 65 and older. In 1880, this ratio was 14 adults for each older person. By 2030, that support ratio will fall to fewer than 3. Not all adults are in the labor market. *IF* labor force participation rates for the population age 20 to 64 are currently at 67%, in just a few years, we will have fewer than 2 workers for each person age 65 and older. And, *IF* a retired person has claims on income equal to three-quarters of the income of the average worker, then nearly 40% of a worker's income might be claimed by a retired person.

The level of aggregate income becomes critical under these circumstances. America's attention for the foreseeable future must be given to increasing the productivity of our economy so that we generate sufficient

TIGHTROPE TO TOMORROW

income that would permit workers to feel comfortable with the sacrifices implied by these data.

To the extent that education is a key component of productivity growth, efforts to improve workforce development are vital. Since the oldest of the baby boomers will turn 65 in less than 10 years, we have little time to make significant progress. Experimental programs and diffused efforts will not do the job of improving the skills of those already in the labor force. Doctrinal disputes among educators will not accelerate the progress needed to have an internationally competitive labor force. Union obstinacy and ineffectual leadership by administrators and public officials will only accelerate an avoidable crisis.

Although we have made changes in structure, curriculum, and financing, the basic forms of education today are consistent with those of the 1880s and 1890s. We still operate through local school systems under state supervision. We continue to rely on the property tax to finance our schools. We progressively add functions and responsibilities to the burden of teaching. To meet the challenges represented by the demographic surge of the 40s, 50s, and early 60s, changes in education are imperative. We do not have the luxury of time.

The Chinese farmer and his family lived in a society of traditional transition. Our demographic history has combined with those long-held American values that have given us dissolving family structures. Together, these forces require that we act boldly to meet a dramatic transition. The comfort and financial security of 70 million persons—our brothers and sisters, and we ourselves—are at risk.

"I could read *before* I went to school," Serina retorted. "My momma taught me how. I was reading to you last summer, way before school started."

Three

Education and the Economy

. . . work should be transfused with intellectual and moral vision and thereby turned into a joy, triumphing over its weariness and its pain.

— Alfred North Whitehead

In the preceding chapter, we established what is well known: America will have many older citizens in the years ahead. And the years ahead are just around the corner.

Older citizens will increase the demand for health care, and they will have expectations of income from public and private sources. Consequently, either we take a larger slice of the existing pie to support the health care and income demands of our older population, or we increase the size of the pie.

But there is an alternative. We can decrease our expectations.

To increase the share of resources going to older Americans, without significant economic growth, will mean continuing the problems of the last few decades. We will be engaged in a battle of redistribution. This can bring the young into conflict with their elders over issues of government taxation and expenditures. It can drive a wedge between the interests of workers and those of stockholders, flaring up as battles over corporate wage and salary policies as well as business investment decisions.

Imagine the debates of the future:

- How much do we tax workers to support the promises of the social security system?
- What portion of health care expenditures should be borne by taxpayers, and what part should be paid by the elderly themselves?

- How much of a corporation's after-tax earnings should be paid out as dividends, and what portion should be retained for investment in future productive capacity?
- Should earnings be taxed at the corporate level and then taxed again when they are received as income by individual dividend recipients?

Surprise! None of these questions is different from the issues we face today. In the future, however, the intensity of the discussion may be much greater as we will have more elderly Americans seeking to exercise their claims on the income generated by workers.

The social security system is clearly understood to be in trouble. The proposed remedies are:

- to increase social security tax rates,
- to increase the base (tax higher incomes),
- to constrain increases (for example, reduce the annual increases associated with the consumer price index),
- to delay the age of retirement (which has advanced from 65 to 67 under provisions put in place several years ago),
- to means-test benefits (decrease payments for persons with incomes above certain levels),
- to invest a portion of the social security trust fund in the stock market,
- to provide individuals with an option to decline participation in the system.

Each of these proposals has already been initiated or may see enactment in the near future. But all involve intergenerational conflict. Already, significant growth in social security, medicare, and medicaid programs have led to public concern about the living standard of the working Americans. We have financed benefits for the elderly with taxes that fall on the income of current wage and salary earners. In the process, we have raised questions about the prospects of today's young adults to achieve the same material benefits as their parents.

The alternative to redistribution is economic growth. A larger pie could be cut along the same lines as the existing pie. But a larger pie offers a greater volume of income to be shared by all. This, of course, sounds fine, but economic growth is not easily attained. In recent years,

America's GDP has grown slowly. And part of that growth may be more apparent than real.

When calculating GDP, we measure only a part of the national economy. Excluded from our economic accounts are services rendered by citizens in their own homes. When you wash your dishes, your clothes, or (if you do) your windows, that effort is not part of our gross domestic product calculation. When you hire someone to do those jobs, that market transaction is part of GDP. We may not have more clean dishes, clothes, or windows, but our GDP is larger. As Americans have substituted market transactions for home-made efforts, GDP has grown. We may not be eating better bread when we buy it in the bakery, but it counts for more.

Any instruction of children provided by parents, grandparents, and other family members is not counted in GDP. We could have a massive effort by parents to increase the readiness of their children for school, and that major increase in labor services would not be part of our Gross Domestic Product.[1]

Whenever our economy seems to be growing too rapidly, there is a danger of inflation. Then the Federal Reserve Board rushes in and clamps down on economic growth by raising interest rates. We salute that effort, but rarely ask why we cannot grow more rapidly.

Other nations are growing faster. But the records of Singapore, Malaysia, or Korea are often dismissed because they are small economies, well behind the U.S. in overall development. We presume there is a growth curve on which our returns are likely to be lower than those of other nations because we are already a large, mature economy. It is another application of the law of diminishing returns as taught in freshman economics classes.

"Now, you read to me," Serina told her grandfather. "No, you read to me," Septum replied. He sounded gruff, but she knew it was all bluff. "I'm not paid to read to you. I'm just supposed to keep you while your mother's off doing whatever she does, and I'm not paid for that either. So you entertain me. Read to me some more. Let's see how good that school is at teaching you to read."

Serina looked sharply at him. "I could read before I went to school. My momma taught me how. I was reading to you last summer, way before school started." Her memory refreshed his, and he nodded in agreement. "So stop talking and read," he urged her.

But how do we jump from one level of potential to another? How do we escape the limitations of low fertility rates and increased leisure? Education is often offered as an answer. Yet, some would argue that we already have reached the point of diminishing returns even with education. They see an "over-educated" America. Anecdotal stories of electrical engineers driving taxi cabs are a delight for those who believe we have already achieved too much of a good thing.

Others will contend that the taxi driver is an anomaly and may be more a reflection of market imperfections than an indicator of over-investment in education. Clearly, we have many taxi drivers who are not capable of doing the tasks of an electrical engineer. Would we be wasting our resources to invest in the education of those workers?

Mark Rosenzweig writes, "the priority that schooling investment should be accorded in a development program whose objective is to maximize economic growth remains unclear."[2] The issue, according to this economics professor from the University of Pennsylvania, is to match schooling with opportunities to learn. He defines learning as "the acquisition of better information as to the most appropriate sets of inputs in a production process."[3] Such knowledge may be obtained from manuals, emulating others, or experimentation. Schooling can enhance the capability of an individual to learn by providing better access to information or a better framework in which information may be synthesized. In an environment of technological or organizational change, the returns from schooling should be higher than in more stable times.

Persons who learn also affect others. If one farmer learns how to use a new seed more effectively, that knowledge is observable by others. To the extent that the learning was aided by schooling, the entire community may benefit from a single person's education. This can lead to under-investment in education as citizens see little reason to participate when the benefits are believed to be available as a spillover or externality.

We see this behavior in many offices where one person may be sent to learn a new software package. The assumption is that this individual will then find ways to use that package and transmit that knowledge to others. It fails, however, to account for the added potential discoveries that additional students might make.

America is in a time of considerable technological change. Our production techniques are being transformed rapidly. Consequently, we should be in a superior position to apply schooling to on-the-job learning.

But has our schooling retarded our growth? John Bishop of Cornell University's Department of Personnel and Human Resource Studies has found that decreased American productivity growth is clearly associated with a decline in academic test scores.[4] Over a thirteen-year period, beginning in 1967 and ending in 1980, measures of general intellectual achievement broke with historic patterns of increase. Bishop does not try to fix blame for this situation. He recognizes that schools have diverse objectives, and forces external to the schools have a considerable bearing on student performance. But he concludes:

> If the rate of gain in the academic achievement of new high school graduates that prevailed between 1948 and 1973 had been maintained, workers would now be 2.9 percent more productive. The effected workers [more recent graduates] will remain in the labor force for 50 years, so [his work] forecasts even larger reductions in productivity in the coming years. Even with an assumption of big gains in academic achievement in the future, the forecast is for a 6.7 percent labor quality shortfall in the year 2010.[5]

Bishop goes on to identify the costs to our society in terms of foregone income, savings, and the profitability of investments. He suggests that the only way to prevent his forecasts from being realized is to break the link between achievement at age 17 and performance as an adult: "This might be accomplished by attracting massive numbers of adults back into school, by expanding educational offerings on television and/or by inducing employers to provide general education to long-term employees."[6]

How do we increase the pie?

The output of an economy is a complex interaction of its physical and human resources. A farmer, his plow, and his land can produce a crop. The more knowledge the farmer has about the weather, insects, diseases, varieties of plants and their patterns of growth, the better are his chances of producing a bigger crop.

But the plow itself is an embodiment of human knowledge. The accumulated knowledge of generations is materialized in the plow. What is known about metal formation and shaping is in the plow. What is known about wood, its varieties and uses, is in the plow. The farmer may not have this knowledge, but the plow maker does.

Americans understand that investment in factories and machinery will help a company produce more of a better product. That investment incorporates the knowledge of humanity, accumulated over centuries. The income which flows from that investment, the returns to capital, are returns to education in its broadest sense, and they continue for an indefinite time into the future. As Martin Weale, the British economist, has stated,

> Because ideas are not lost once they are implemented, such a situation means that benefit from education accrues not only to those currently alive who are not educated, but also to future generations. As such, it suggests that part of the burden of current education should be borne by future generations. One way of doing this is to maintain a national debt.[7]

This is not how politicians, parents, and students normally discuss the economic returns to education. They think about the gains to the student. This is reinforced by our persistent focus on the differential between the income of persons with one level of schooling and the income of those with more years of schooling.

Regular press releases from the U.S. Bureau of the Census and other agencies tell us that education is a key factor in differentiating one person from another in the marketplace. Income differences between persons with different levels of education attainment are reported regularly. The assumption is that more education leads to more income for the recipient of that education.

In addition, we are ready to recognize that nations with higher levels of education attainment by their citizens generally have higher incomes.

Cause and effect are quickly linked: the education system is the key to economic growth.

Critics will differentiate between education and time spent in schools. They will argue that schooling is attendance, not necessarily the acquisition of knowledge. Degrees and certificates awarded may not correlate with either substantive understanding or the ability to use knowledge in routine circumstances or creative opportunities.

At the level of the economy in general, education can be imported. It does not have to be produced domestically. The economic boom in much of Southeast Asia is the result of an inflow of capital goods, machines that embody knowledge produced in other countries. America's own economic development was often the result of clever Yankees appropriating ideas and processes from Europeans. We did not hesitate to steal ideas in those days; we were not always as concerned with intellectual property rights as we are today.

Likewise, income can be imported. When Americans buy stock in corporations that own assets abroad, they acquire rights to the income produced by those assets. Thus, a citizen of Cleveland can, through stock ownership, secure a claim on income produced by the labor of workers in India as well as in Indiana.

But for a nation the size of the United States, given our comparatively advanced economy, we might

"There's no point to investing in America and the education of Americans, if we can lay claim to income made by foreigners through stock ownership," Sheldon announced.

"There's no point talking to you, if we can get an equally intelligent opinion from a reupholstered settee," Septum responded. *"You forget that when Americans produce goods in this country, we get spinoffs of production . . . jobs for our people, revenues for our businesses, and taxes for our governments."*

"Protectionism," cried Sheldon. *"Knee-jerk nonsense."* Septum, too, raised his voice. *"Nobody's talking about keeping foreign goods out. I'm only pointing out that there are benefits, beyond prices paid by consumers, to be had from making things here rather than there."*

"Under conditions of full employment —" Sheldon attempted a rejoinder. *"Full buckets of hogwash,"* Septum bellowed, drowning out the man he thought of as "the pariah with a pencil."*

do best by investing in the Creation, Organization, and Dissemination of knowledge. This C.O.D. economy stresses research and development expenditures. Basic and applied efforts in universities, corporate laboratories, and government facilities can be augmented by the less organized geniuses of the basement and garage culture.

The C.O.D. education economy also builds education capital. Teachers have done this for generations. Lecture notes are the way instructors organize a body of knowledge. Those working in the right environment, with very good notes, and some talent, can then convert these personal assets into textbooks. Today, however, the organization of knowledge is being transformed by computer technologies.

Computers are also at the heart of future dissemination modes. When few could read, the textbook was not an efficient dissemination tool. As reading became more prevalent, the textbook became a dominant means of disseminating knowledge. With growing computer literacy and the spread of computer ownership across more income groups, new means of disseminating knowledge will restructure formal and informal education.

In addition, we can increase the output of the proposed economy by increasing the capability of currently underutilized resources. Those Americans who graduated from or left high school between 1970 and 1990 are at the heart of today's labor force. They are, roughly speaking, between the ages of 25 and 44. To the extent that they are illiterate, inadequately prepared in arithmetic, algebra, and communication skills, and deficient in their knowledge of history and geography, they have been shortchanged by the education system.

Even if these former students have higher levels of achievement than depicted above, is that adequate for the years ahead? Sheldon and Suzannah Seriatim may have learned everything taught to them in the mid-1960s, but that may be far less than their children are learning today in the same schools. The re-entry of adults to our education systems may be the best hope of the nation for economic growth.

What gains in productivity are possible, if we enhance the education of those persons 25 to 44 years of age? In 1994, there were 83.5 million persons in that age group, of whom 10.4 million had not completed high school. In addition, 28.3 million men and women were high school graduates, but had no further education.[8] In sum, there are more than 38 million Americans who are the products of our local school systems who may be subject to a product recall. But these numbers neglect those who went into the higher education system. Can we assume that they are adequately prepared and sufficiently functional in today's internationally competitive work force?

Not all of these 83.5 million Americans are in the labor force. Many of those not working or seeking employment are, however, parents. Whether employed or not, this group of Americans molds the attitudes and capabilities of the next generation, while providing the energy and muscle for today's economy.

If the American economy is to grow rapidly in the years ahead, we may need to bring this group of Americans together with our school systems. This does not mean putting adults into the primary and secondary classrooms. Rather, it may involve taking the schools to their homes, their shopping malls, and their places of employment.

Education in America has been bound by geography and physical capital. We are organized in school districts, many of which have their origins in political subdivisions (cities, townships, counties). These bureaucratic entities own buildings, and, in our minds, education is associated with these structures. We tend to view our school buildings as our primary education resource.

School districts may be seen as employers of education resources, of which teachers have been the most important. Where those teachers practice their skills is secondary. Face-to-face interactions have been the most efficient means of bringing students and teachers together, although tomorrow, interactive telecommunications may be more efficient. And while that is distasteful to many, others see in this new technology the liberation of education from its historic limitations.

This view, which places the teacher at the center of the education process, is consistent with our rhetoric, if not with our practices. But teachers are not in control of education. Power rests with the state legislatures, the state departments of education, and local school boards.

Teachers, as employees, have organized to deal with these many powerful authorities. These teacher organizations, whether they be called unions or professional associations, are identified and vilified as a major retarding force in American education. Their political power is envied and perhaps overstated by their enemies. And they do not have universal support among teachers when they attempt to achieve their goals by coercion, exclusive bargaining rights, and mandatory membership fees.

Whatever we may think of teacher unions, they are a rational response to a complex organization of resources. If we look at education as an industry, we would start by asking,

Who is the customer?
Who are the suppliers?
What is being sold?

Many Americans believe that the customers are the parents of the children who attend the schools. Some would consider the student to be the customer. The suppliers are the school organizations, who employ specialized labor (teachers) to deliver education services and general labor to deliver supplementary supporting services (transportation, lunches, etc.).

Education services direct the student's attention to a set of skills and a body of knowledge. They also assist the student in mastering those skills and retaining that body of knowledge. Reading and writing are such skills. Historical facts are a body of knowledge. Critical reading of history is an augmentation of a basic skill applied to a specific body of knowledge.

In American public education, the consumer does not purchase these services. Taxpayers pay for the services. Consumers pay primarily by devoting time to using the services. The time of the students and their parents is their direct contribution made to the education process. If all taxpayers were parents, we would not have to distinguish between the two sets in the population. But in America today, only 35% of all households have children under age 18.[9]

Since taxpayers are voters, they tend to control the decision-making processes of elected bodies (legislatures and school boards). Parents (consumers) and teachers (the primary suppliers) have less influence than taxpayer-voters on how much education will be produced or the nature of that education.

Hence, if education is important to the nation's economic growth, a system of education should be fostered which benefits, and is seen to benefit, the general public as much as, if not more than, students and teachers. Education systems, not necessarily school systems, need to be developed to increase the ability of Americans to generate the income from which taxes and dividends can be drawn. Then, the resources of our public education systems would be applied to more than the traditional population of young people.

"Sheldon and you," he sneered and shifted his rocker to the right, clearing his line of sight, "are know-nothings."

Four

Alternative Organizations of Education

I think the conception of a dog who talks — and then turns out to be such a crashing bore that they have to lock him away so they won't be obliged to listen to him, is — well glorious that's all. You have to love dogs before you can go on to the step of taking them down, understandingly.

—Dorothy Parker

The operation, control, and financing of economic activities are separable. Septum Sixpack gives his granddaughter money so that she may enjoy the regional amusement park. Septum's daughter, Suzannah, determines when little Serina may visit JollyLand, with whom, and under what restrictions. The actual trip is organized and conducted by a neighbor.

This separation of financing, control, and operation also occurs frequently in the public sector. The state may require that restaurants follow certain public health standards. Cities and counties are mandated to provide inspections, but the state provides no funding for these services. With local property tax funds, the city hires a private firm to conduct the inspections. Control is with the state, financing is at the local level, and operations are private.

Much of the highly publicized drive toward privatization in government is little more than a return of operations to the private sector, while maintaining control and financing in the public sector. Garbage collection is an example. It is normally financed through the general revenues of local governments. But should government employees pick up the trash, or should that service be provided by private haulers? After experience with the potential for graft and political favoritism, private trash collection was discontinued in many American cities during the early part of this century. Those lessons being forgotten, or never learned, we are moving again toward private collection services.

By and large, housing is financed and operated privately. The public sector does have some control, however, through zoning and building codes on several aspects of the structure and its use. In a few instances, government has owned and operated housing units. But government's chief role in housing has been through financing. America subsidizes housing, particularly for the middle- and upper-income groups, through mortgage interest and property tax subsidies under the Internal Revenue Code. Of course, most Americans will deny that they live in publicly subsidized homes.

Primary and secondary education in America is financed largely through the public sector, with state and local governments sharing both the financing and the control, while operations are almost universally local. It could be very different.

Under what conditions should financing, control, and operations be lodged with which form and level of organization? What should be in the public sector and what in the private sector, and at what level in each sector?

These are questions that cannot be answered by empirical tests alone. There are philosophical as well as economic issues involved. Often, garbage smells, and accumulations of rotten animal and vegetable matter on your property can become a health problem to others. The existence of negative or unwanted externalities leads us to intervention by government. We may love our neighbors, but can we trust them to dispose of their waste products appropriately?

At what level of government should regulations be made about garbage? Do we need a national garbage czar? Once, we believed that trash collection and disposal was a local matter. But with interstate shipments of garbage, the federal government is being brought into the act. Senators from garbage-receiving areas are trying to limit commerce in trash.

Many Americans are convinced that the smaller the unit of operations and control, the better the service will be. We accept that there may be economies of scale that make large organizations capable of producing at lower unit costs than smaller entities. But we don't like it.

We also believe that the nearer to home we can place the locus of control, the better will be our chances of achieving our objectives. Distant private sector employees or government bureaucrats, hiding behind layers of organization, are the fiends envisioned when we discuss big business or state or federal operations. Local may be inept, but it is ours. We can easily badger a local person in the office, at the grocery, or on the way to church. A state or federal bureaucrat, the employee of some megacorporation, is beyond our personal in-your-face wrath.

Large scale operations may be able to attract more qualified personnel than smaller efforts, but the risks are great. If a poor decision is made at a small scale, fewer persons will be harmed than if an incompetent functionary promulgates a national order. The fallibility of us all deters us from accepting centralized decision making. We subscribe to the view of Friedrich Hayek, one of the most influential economists and moral philosophers of the 20th century, who wrote that "the recognition of the insuperable limits to his knowledge ought indeed to teach the student of society a lesson in humility which should guard him against becoming an accomplice in men's fatal striving to control society. . . ."[1]

Although many of these matters can be examined through empirical studies, evidence is never as convincing as passion. And the evidence is often confusing. Are there economies of scale in education? And if there are savings to be had from large schools, do they exceed the value of non-economic factors such as pride and community identity? In some circumstances, we permit economic factors to have the preeminent position in our decision making. At other times, we honor the diverse criteria people have for choosing one alternative over another.

The distribution of benefits and costs can be as important as the overall picture. If the benefits are largely limited to one set of persons, we often believe they should pay for the services. If the costs are limited to a narrow group of persons, they will want to have control as well as the honor of financing the service. However, if they can retain the control and shift the burden of financing elsewhere, that option will be preferred.

Most consumer spending is believed to generate benefits that are limited to the individual or household. We call these *private goods*. We ask individuals or households to pay for them. The pizza and beer our friend Septum Sixpack buys falls into this class of goods. No one else is going to benefit from the sausage and the suds other than Septum and his guests.

In some instances, however, we pay for such goods and services through public monies or charitable giving. These are described as *merit goods*. They are private in nature, but we want people to have them. We worry that, if left to their own devices, people would not spend enough on them. Health care expenditures may fall into this category. We fear that the poor, the elderly, and the young may neglect their own welfare because of the expense of health care or because they are ignorant and, hence, indifferent to the consequences of neglect. Our concern is for the well-being of others. It is born mainly of our compassion and only partly from our fears of communicable diseases. We do not dwell on the health consequences for us if the broken hip of an elderly person is unattended. We do not fear that we will be infected when we see a child burned over half her body. We relate to the pain of others.

Beyond these private goods and services are those which have major externalities. They often fall into the public sector. Consumers may not choose enough of a service with positive externalities because they only consider the benefits they gain, not the total benefits generated by the action. Mosquito control is an example. If it costs $10 per treatment to spray your property to control these pests, you will spend up to the point where the increment in expenditure equals the gain to you from another application. Your costs and your preferences alone decide how mosquito abatement will be undertaken.

But your neighbors also benefit from that spraying; this makes the service a *public good*. If they were invited to pay for that service as well, then the amount spent would be determined by the benefits to all, not merely by those benefits you alone realize.

In education, we often choose projects we believe are "good for our children." In the past few years, we have been most concerned about the

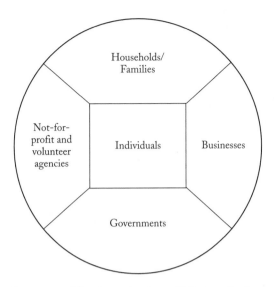

Figure 4.1 The Organization of Modern Society

returns to education in the form of future earnings for the student. But it is appropriate to ask, Is this good for society at large?

Haveman and Wolfe, professors at the University of Wisconsin in Madison, have cataloged the evidence of non-market effects of schooling, many of which are external and can be considered public goods. The list is an impressive array of factors with somewhat less impressive evidence. That is, we can attest to the benefits, but it is difficult to prove their magnitudes.[2] Yet, "once one accepts that there may be external benefits which do accrue to education which are not measured in the marketplace, then the case for government intervention in the market for education becomes overwhelming. . . ."[3]

Now let's consider education within this context.

Education is provided by schools, but it need not be. In the U.S. today, most schools are in the public sector; they are part of government. But they need not be. Schools could be, and through history have been, operated under many different organizational forms.

Human societies develop relationships among the four sectors that constitute the framework within which individuals function. (See *Figure 4.1*.)

The most basic organization of human activity is *the household.* Here, provisions can be made for all essential wants as well as for the continuation of the species. Education is easily provided by adults to children in this setting. Advocates of home schooling seek a return to this most basic organization for the provision of education.

The advantage of home schooling is the control it gives parents over the education of their children. The disadvantages start with the opportunity costs of the parent providing that schooling. That is, parents could be doing something else. They could be weeding the garden or out in the marketplace earning money. Another disadvantage arises from the limited education options available when a student has only one teacher over an extended period of time. Economies of scale also broaden the education options of the child in a larger group. More education resources are likely to be available in the school library than at home, although the public library and the Internet provide the home school with supplemental resources at low cost in today's world.

Parents are likely to prepare their children to be like themselves. In past centuries, children learned the trade of the parents. The genetic code ensured the succession of physical traits and home schooling became a social and economic mold.

Businesses evolve from households. Individuals with a talent for baking will provide their neighbors with goodies in exchange for the

"You will not," Septum said emphatically. "I will if I want to," his daughter replied, equally determined. "You will not endanger the mind of my granddaughter by attempting home schooling," he said, and turned away from Suzannah.

She moved her chair so she was now directly in front of Septum's rocker, obstructing his view of the house across the street. "Sheldon and I know what we want her to learn."

"Sheldon and you," he sneered and shifted his rocker to the right, clearing his line of sight, "are know-nothings. You want to perpetuate your narrow-mindedness, your mean-spirited selfish ideas. Serina deserves the benefit of teachers who have seen something of the world, read some of the great ideas of history, dreamed of more than a bongo party on the beach. She should have access to ideas that contrast with those of her parents so she isn't just another peanut butter cookie from your kitchen."

products of other households. Specialization in production by individuals in the household leads to the formation of separate entities, which we call firms. The good baker opens a bakery.

Education can be provided in the business firm when an individual is ready to assume tasks that contribute to the success of the firm. Apprenticeships offer young people opportunities to learn a trade, once they have acquired the fundamental skills necessary to function in the ordinary life of the community. Apprenticeships increase upward mobility or, at minimum, diversification of the family's economic opportunities. In the past, they served as a form of social and economic interbreeding between households. Sending your children to work in the next village in the 17th century was like sending them away to college today—it increased access to a wider gene pool.

But what incentive does the master have to provide the apprentice with skills that are not directly applicable to the activities of the firm? What is the contribution to the bottom line of educating the whole person? Training programs provide skills that help one earn a living. Education helps one live a life. The employer, presumably, has little interest in broadening the horizons of the worker, particularly if the worker might then take off for that more distant horizon.

Schools themselves can be organized as businesses when individuals choose to specialize in education services. We see this in its most private form when one neighbor baby-sits for another. From this custodial acorn mighty academic oaks might grow.

More often, we have seen schools develop as specialized, ancillary activities of *not-for-profit agencies*. Just as households and businesses exist to provide benefits to their members, not-for-profit organizations are an alternative means formed by communities to provide benefits for specific groups. Churches, Rotary Clubs, the Manufacturers Association, and the Red Cross are neither businesses nor households. They exist to provide persons who share a common set of beliefs or interests with a set of specialized services that are not readily produced in the home or business environment.

Today, schools are organized by not-for-profit organizations when they can efficiently offer instruction beyond that which is in the domain of the individual household or business establishment. For example, parents may not have a good grasp of arithmetic, and it is clear to them that a specialist, a teacher, could do a better job of conveying this subject to their children than they could at home. Likewise, a business may not feel that it would benefit directly from teaching elements of civics to its apprentices, but sees the value to itself and society of having the elements of democratic institutions taught to young people.

In colonial America and during most of the 19th century, churches dominated the education landscape. Religious instruction was considered basic to the development of a moral society and public funds were used to support education in religious institutions, but often with great conflict.

Public education in its earliest forms was instruction outside the home in an academy. These academies often were philanthropic organizations, intended to provide instruction to those who did not have a church affiliation.

Governments are organized to protect the lives and property of households and their extensions—firms. Throughout history, there have been other groups of households ready to take what they want by force. To assure a community that goods and services will be transferred according to established rules and customs, governments become specialists in protecting households and firms from strangers and neighbors who would appropriate resources by force. The baker may be willing to trade bread for wine or just a friendly smile, but securing resources by force or stealth is universally unpopular.

How then do governments form schools? What is being protected? The Massachusetts School Act of November 11, 1647, was protecting the colony from "that old deluder, Satan, [who would] keep men from the knowledge of the Scriptures."[4]

One hundred and forty years later, "the essentials of [Noah] Webster's version of a truly American education would be given in local public schools . . . conducted at least four months a year by the most respected and best informed men of the community."[5] And Webster's hope was that "the rough manners of the wilderness should be softened and the principles of virtue and good behavior inculcated."[6]

Fifty years later, "the need to discipline an urban workforce intersected with the fear of crime and poverty and the anxiety about cultural diversity to hasten the establishment of public educational systems."[7]

As Henry Barnard reported to the Connecticut General Assembly ten years before the Civil War,

> No one at all familiar with the deficient household arrangements and deranged machinery of domestic life, of the extreme poor, and ignorant, to say nothing of the intemperate — of the examples of rude manners, impure and profane language, and all the vicious habits of low-bred idleness, which abound in certain sections of all populous districts — can doubt, that it is better for children to be removed as early and as long as possible from such scenes and examples. . . .[8]

Yes, government has been called upon to protect us from evil in its many forms, from forces that would disrupt society, and from that unspecified portion of the population that would deny the rewards of life to those justly deserving them.

But which government? Our history, as Michael Katz, director of the Urban Studies program at the University of Pennsylvania, reports, is replete with conflicting views. There was, in his words, "democratic localism," operating against a "paternalistic" view. Many contemporary citizens would be comfortable with the sentiment that

> government had as a "right no control over our opinions, literary, moral, political, philosophical, or religious." On the contrary, its task was "to reflect, not to lead, nor to create the will." Government thus "must not be installed as the educator of the people."[9]

Local control fostered "the idiosyncratic character of community schools shaped by local parents that gave the common school its 'charm.'"[10]

In opposition are those citizens who see education as a social necessity to preserve and advance the general welfare. The benefits to the individual are supplemented, and perhaps exceeded, by the security afforded to all members of the larger community. Katz reports that taxation represented "a solemn compact between the citizen and State"; the citizen contributed in order to protect his "person" and secure his "property." The "State, compelling such contributions, is under reciprocal obligation" to compel attendance at schools. Thus compulsory education became "a duty to the taxpayer."[11]

━━━━━━━━

"Not around here you won't," Septum said. "Yes, I will," I insisted. "I'm going to ask every person on the block to sign this petition to have the schools adopt a new social studies curriculum that emphasizes teaching economics."

"Whose economics?" Septum asked. "Are you going to get them teaching Marx? Are they going to teach anything about unions? Or are they going to teach free-market prepackaged pap from the chamber pot of commerce?"

"That's not fair," I protested. "You bet it's not fair," he shot back, not letting me finish my thought. "Our schools aren't fair because they don't teach enough about the different ideas folks have had on organizing society. All they teach is what the fool school board thinks is safe."

"But that's the whole idea of locally controlled schools," I argued. "Local control," he snapped, "local capitulation to mediocrity is more like it. Bunch of conformists is all we got on the school board. Not a one has read a book worth reading in twenty years. Just a bunch . . ."

I had to leave before the diatribe was complete.

In our times, we would add that each citizen is potentially productive. Education, we believe, enriches and extends the potential of each individual. The neglect of that potential is a waste of a national resource, denying to all the benefits each individual is capable of producing for the common good.

If an individual, the parents of that person, or the community in which he or she resides fails to develop that potential, the nation suffers. First, the nation has less valuable output produced by that person over his or her lifetime (including services rendered at home and not valued in the marketplace, such as child care). As stated earlier, we all have claims on the income generated by others. Thus, it is in our interest to see that our fellow citizens are capable of producing income within the bounds of their capacity.

Second, should the individual, by choice or chance, become unable to provide for his or her own well-being, our social values call on all citizens, through welfare and charitable deeds, to provide re-

TIGHTROPE TO TOMORROW

sources to that person. This protection, this social insurance, involves mutual obligation. To qualify for these transfers from the rest of us, it is reasonable to expect all citizens, while able and competent, to participate fully in the education system which will enhance their capabilities.

The issue, then, becomes one of defining "community." Parental control, local control, even state control of education diminishes or discounts the complex connectivity of modern society. If the consequences (benefits) of education are limited to the student and those in his or her immediate household, then parental control of education is most logical. If the locality alone supports the schools and the benefits are all contained in that area, local control is warranted.

But in our times, states have assumed a major role in financing education and the benefits, extending well beyond the borders of the school district or state, are shared by the student and a much wider society. Therefore, it becomes timely and perhaps necessary to consider a broader program of financial support for schools and a greater role for the nation in the governance of education.

"Precision is rarely needed for understanding," Suzannah replied. "You need to be current or exact only when you're making a critical decision."

Five

How Do We Pay for Education?

It is sometimes said that the economist has a special obligation to make himself understood because his subject is of such great and popular importance. By this rule the nuclear physicist would have to speak in monosyllables.

— John Kenneth Galbraith

Current practices

In the mid-1990s, about 50 million American children attended elementary and secondary classes. Nearly 90% of these students were in more than 85,000 public schools. In 1995, the 2.5 million students who graduated from our high schools equaled 73.4% of the 17-year-old population.

Romantics will be disappointed to learn that fewer than 450 one-teacher schools remain in our nation. Public education is organized in almost 15,000 school districts or corporations, served by approximately 5 million employees.[1] Half of these employees were assigned as classroom teachers. Seventy of the school corporations have responsibility for more than 50,000 students each.

In the 1993 school year, public schools spent nearly $254 billion; this included nearly $221 billion for current operations, $23 billion in capital outlay, and $5.4 billion in interest on debt.[2] That same year, public elementary and secondary schools had revenues of $248.5 billion.[3] Not included in these figures are the sums borrowed during the year by school corporations in the nation's capital markets, the sum of their outstanding debt, the magnitudes of their pension plans (funded and unfunded). That's a fair sized industry.

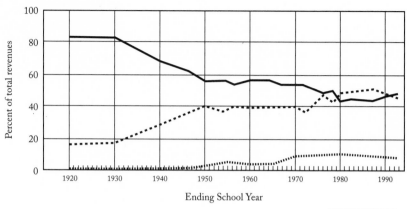

Figure 5.1   Education Revenues by Source
Elementary and secondary education

⋯⋯ Federal
- - - State
—— Local

Where does all this money come from? Roughly speaking, local and state governments divide the responsibility for funding education. In academic year 1992-93, the federal government provided just 6.9% of the support for elementary and secondary schools in America. Localities came up with 47.4% of the total and the states contributed 45.6%.[4]

"You can't have local schools unless you have local money," Septum was declaring as I climbed the steps to his porch. "Federal aid, state funding just means an end to local control. And then what do you have?" he asked without expecting an answer.

"I'll tell you," he continued. "You'll have the feds and the state guys telling us what to teach in our own schools."

"Why not?" I asked. "Is the geography, arithmetic, music, biology we teach here different from that taught in another district or another state?"

"Local values," was his terse reply. "Local baloney," was my impolite rejoinder.

Once upon a time, local sources accounted for more than 80% of public school funding. (See *Figure 5.1.*) The trauma of the Great Depression in the 1930s increased state government participation from less than 17% (in 1930) to more than 30% (in 1940). By 1950, the states were contributing nearly 40% to public schools, and federal funding was approaching 3%. A historic

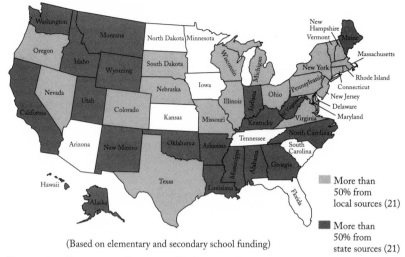

(Based on elementary and secondary school funding)

More than 50% from local sources (21)

More than 50% from state sources (21)

Figure 5.2   Dominant Sources of Education Revenues, 1993
By state

point was reached in 1975, when local funding fell below 50% for the first time, as federal financing reached 9%, and the states picked up 42% of the burden.

Over the past 20 years, there was only a slight change in these relationships. In 1992-93, the federal portion was less than 7%. The remaining 93% was divided almost equally between the states and the local units, but the differences among states were enormous.

In 21 of the 50 states, local sources were dominant, that is, they equaled or exceeded 50% of total revenue. (See *Figures 5.2* and *5.3.*) New Hampshire was at one extreme, with nearly 89% of public school revenues derived from local sources.[5] State sources were dominant in another 21 states, with Hawaii, as the extreme case, providing over 90% of all public school revenues for its distinctive statewide school district.[6]

During the same year, federal contributions to school revenues exceeded 10% in only nine states. (See *Figure 5.4.*) Poverty programs and special populations (including children on federal facilities) are the chief determinants of federal funding. Connecticut and New Jersey, our two wealthiest states (as measured by per capita personal income) were among the seven states with less than 5% of their funds derived from federal sources.

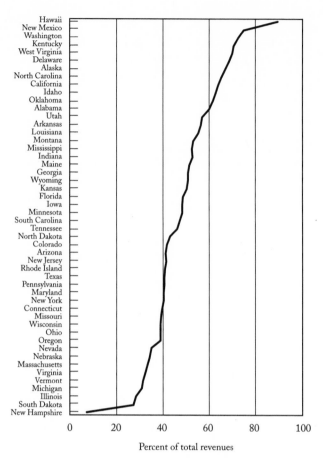

Figure 5.3 State Support of Education, 1993
Elementary and secondary schools

On the surface, states and localities seemed to share equally in financing public education. Nationally, states bore 45.6% of the cost, and localities came in at 47.4%. (See again *Figure 5.1.*) As is often the case, however, this aggregate figure hid and distorted reality.

When all the states are considered as an aggregate, the difference between these two percentages was just 1.8 points. But only two states (Minnesota at 1.1 points and Tennessee at 1.5) were actually below that national figure. Iowa and North Dakota were right on the national mark. The other 46 states had greater differences between the state and local shares.

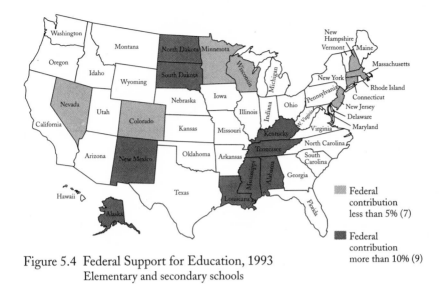

Figure 5.4 Federal Support for Education, 1993
Elementary and secondary schools

The average for all states, as compared with the national aggregate number (1.8), was a difference of 24 percentage points. As seen in *Figure 5.5,* 11 states had differences of 33 or more points, and only a dozen states came in under 10 points. Therefore, it must have been difficult for citizens of the different states, or their governors, to discuss education finance from a common point of view.

Clearly, Hawaii and New Hampshire were at the extremes. They may rank 40th and 41st in population, but they continue to be ideal examples of opposites. New Hampshire is one of the original colonies; Hawaii is the most recent entry to the Union. New Hampshire is virtually homogeneous in racial composition; Hawaii is dramatically diverse. New Hampshire's population is growing at one quarter the rate of Hawaii's. While a spine of mountains divides New Hampshire, the state is relatively compact. Nearly 320 miles, by air, separates Hilo from Kapaa in Hawaii.

Each of these elements of geography and population would seem to suggest highly localized public education in Hawaii and more state involvement in New Hampshire. But the opposite is true. History, tradition, philosophy, and, possibly, inertia made New Hampshire the state with the highest percent of local support for schools in the country.

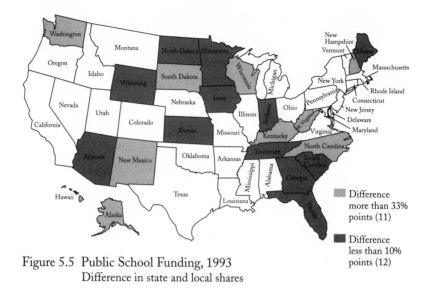

Figure 5.5 Public School Funding, 1993
Difference in state and local shares

Difference more than 33% points (11)

Difference less than 10% points (12)

Could we expect citizens of Hawaii and New Hampshire to agree on a national school financing formula? Could we expect New Mexico and Kentucky, where state support exceeds 67%, to have views that are congruent with Virginia and Vermont, where the state's share is only 32%?

The diversity of public school finance practices in the United States leads experts in the subject to deny their expertise. But experts, political leaders, newspaper editors, and social critics are in agreement that schools are becoming more expensive, and they do not seem to deliver what we want, if we even know what we want. As a recent Brookings report states, "Even a cursory examination of the historical patterns of student performance and school finance highlights a central mystery of the education debate. The nation is spending more and more to achieve results that are no better, and perhaps worse."[7]

Performance and education finance

The debate over education's performance clouds discussions of education finance. Plus, complex issues are not readily discussed in a nation attuned

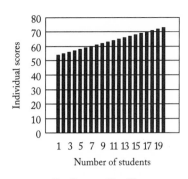
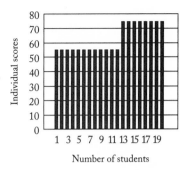

Test Scores at East Elementary
School average = 63.5
Students scoring 75 or better = 0%

Test Scores at West Elementary
School average = 63.0
Students scoring 75 or better = 40%

Figure 5.6 Comparative Test Scores

to 30-second sound bites. And, the people who enjoy discussing them often are not required to provide solutions. (Perhaps the process of providing solutions to complex issues reduces the enjoyment one gets from discussing them.)

Reforming our schools and reforming the way in which we finance education should be separable topics. But, as in most issues, they are interwoven. As Mary Fulton, a policy analyst at the Education Commission of the States, writes,

Some judges actually are defining [an] "efficient" and "adequate" education and charging lawmakers with designing a funding [formula], and possibly an entire education system, that supports this definition. The striking observation is that the courts' description of adequacy focuses on student results—the skills and competencies which an education should provide—rather than solely on inputs—the specific components that must go into an education system.[8]

This move to tie education financing to performance is part of a historic shift that characterizes our times. We look at outcomes. We don't ask what the student-teacher ratio is; we want to know test results. Although it has many virtues, this approach can be a convenient diversion.

It is easy to become tied up in debates about performance standards. Whose performance?

Are we most concerned about the performance

of the individual student, or
of some aggregate of students at
the school,
the district,
the state, or
the national level?

It is easy to devise standards and dispute alternative interpretations of results. Consider the following example:

Twenty students at East and twenty at West Elementary schools take an examination. Their scores are shown in *Figure 5.6*. If our concern is at the level of the student, we might choose to look at what percent of students achieve a score of 75 or better on a given examination. None of the students at the East Elementary School achieve this standard. At the West School, however, 40% of the students hit this level. On this student-based criterion, West is superior.

But we could make East the winner, if we choose a minimum performance standard. When we look at the percent of students with a score under 60, East has only 30%, while West has 60% under that magic level.

But if we measure performance at the school level, we could argue they are even, with East only slightly ahead. The average score at East is 63.5, while West is right behind at 63.

And then inquiring minds will want to know, What is performance? Is it

- achieving a defined level of a given measure, or
- the increment (change) in an attribute over time?

How can we choose between East and West when we haven't even begun to gather data on changes over time?

In the past, educators and the public focused on inputs. Were the teachers certified? How many books were in the library? Was there a library?

Now, we are to be concerned about the performance of teachers. We hear that pay increases should be tied, not to years of experience or certification, but to test results of students. I suspect that many teachers look at this as the equivalent of turning the fire department over to a committee of confirmed arsonists.

Schools at all levels used to be accredited on the basis of inputs. That, too, is changing, but it is not simplifying the life of either those providing accreditation or those seeking it.

Inputs have long served as proxies for outputs. Often, we felt more confidence in having judgments made on the basis of inputs so that we would not risk undesirable outcomes. For example, we want restaurants to meet certain health codes. We want the food prepared from non-toxic ingredients and under conditions of good sanitation. We could, however, have output measurements alone and do away with intrusive inspections, as some ultra-empiricists (read: conservatives, if you want a political interpretation) have suggested. After we have experienced a certain number of deaths and/or serious gastronomical disturbances, consumers would learn to stay away.

Output measurement is necessarily after-the-fact. Parents, employers, or whoever we consider to be the "customers" of the school are not always going to be willing to accept output reports when the costs of remediation are high and the risks of low-quality outputs can be assessed from information about inputs.

"You'll have to do this over," Sheldon told his wife. "You can't submit this report to the school board with old numbers."

"That's foolish," Suzannah replied. "I got the best numbers available when I put that report together."

"Listen, numbers are my business," the accountant replied, stiffening his back. "You can't go into that meeting without the latest numbers. A bad number with a current date is better than a good number that is a week old."

"That's dumb," his wife countered. "Numbers only give people an idea of what's going on. If something changes slowly, older numbers can be as useful as newer ones. Precision is rarely needed for understanding. You need to be current or exact only when you're making a critical decision. Otherwise, you can overinvest in data. You may need precision if you're going to build a bookcase or a bridge, but we drive to work without knowing how many inches are between here and there."

"Do what you will," Sheldon replied, "but you'll get criticized. Trust me, I'm a CPA."

None of these considerations invalidate the call for performance measurement and the use of such measurements in the allocation of resources. Rather, they are intended to show just a few of the most elementary reasons why such measures are difficult to adopt.

But they are being adopted, with and without their difficulties. After the State Supreme Court declared existing school district boundaries and the patterns of governance and school finance unconstitutional in 1989, the Kentucky Education Reform Act (KERA) set up a system to identify both successful schools and those in crisis.

"The feds put much more money into the schools than is normally realized," Sheldon said. *"And how would you know?" Suzannah challenged.*

"National Center for Education Statistics Report 95-215 says that if you include on-budget and off-budget support, over $100 billion went to education in FY '95," he reported. "Fascinating," she replied. "Yes," he continued, "and no one can argue reasonably that Washington controls our schools because they put money into them."

"Intriguing," she yawned. "Perhaps the feds have little control because thus far only one-fifth of that $100 billion goes to local education agencies."

"How did you know that?" he demanded. She replied, as she rose to leave the room. "You talk in your sleep . . . which helps me fall back to sleep since you never have anything interesting to say."

The reward system is to be based on the following: (1) a school is to be the unit of accountability; (2) school success is to be determined by measuring improvement on the state assessment over a two-year period; (3) a school is to be rewarded for increasing the proposition of successful students, including those students who are at risk of school failure; (4) a threshold level for school improvement is to be established for each school to determine the amount of success needed for a school to receive a reward; (5) the threshold definition must establish the percent of increase required in a school's proportion of successful students as compared to its present proportions.[9]

This ambitious program is a major attempt to link school funding to performance and output measures.

As consumers, we regularly use information about both inputs and outputs. Some health-conscious consumers will buy bread because it was made with unbleached flour and no saturated fats. They expect certain outputs from using these inputs. Others will buy a car because of the way in which it rides when they take it on the freeway. They are testing performance. They do not know, and may be indifferent to, the working conditions under which the car was manufactured, the alcohol level of the workers when they mounted the wheels, or any other input considerations. If the wheels do not fall off at 65 mph, it is good enough.

We may then ask, Why do the schools have to go to such lengths to measure performance? And why do they want to use, as in Kentucky, examinations which are current indicators, when the output and the performance about which we are concerned are more long-term matters?

Would it not be more appropriate to look at the former students of a given program ten years later and see how they are performing? Yes, but there are many intervening factors. It is far easier to test a current tenth grader than to find that same person several years later and see if a product recall is in order.

If education is to be a crucial means to help the nation increase profits and productivity, leading to increased income and services for the elderly, then the performance measures we want are not to be found by testing 4th, 8th, and 12th grade students today in Kentucky. Instead, our concern must be to improve education as it takes place and to take those steps necessary to make restitution to those inadequately served by our schools in the past. This will require a reconsideration of whom the schools serve and how they deliver education services.

Other issues in financing education

In each state, there is one person who is said to know and understand the state school aid formula. Over the years, states have devised elaborate—no, Byzantine—means of allocating state funds. Why? Because state legislators are good people who want to do the right thing for their constituents, they are willing to include conditions and exceptions which mirror the complex world in which we live.

Hence, the starting point of state aid, providing assistance to assure every child a minimum level of education resources, is quickly turned into a fiscal collage of jagged concepts and well-worn homilies. Basic or foundation grants to school corporations are quickly modified to recognize the ability of the local unit to support that foundation itself. Suddenly, we are equalizing the resources available and considering the tax base of the locality, plus the rate applied to that base by the local district. Our focus thus shifts from securing sufficient education resources to testing the political will of localities and compensating for economic conditions beyond the control of the local schools. We would never want to give a penny to the undeserving!

But we cannot stop there. We must consider, as well, the impediments to education that may be met in each school corporation. Only state legislatures would actually try to assist those districts in which students have to go to school uphill in both directions.

Such cynicism aside, state equalization efforts are successful, according to a recent study from the National Center for Education Statistics:

> The distribution of public education resources is substantially more nearly equal than wealth measured by housing values, and somewhat less varied than wealth measured by household income.
>
> State public education allocation systems are the primary equalizing factors of education resources, with some additional equalization resulting from the various federal funding programs.[10]

"None of this makes any sense," Septum muttered as he read through Serina's homework. "When I went to school, you learned things your parents knew, and they could test you on them without looking up the answers. There are countries in this book that I never heard of and see no need to know anything about."

This does not suggest that the funding levels are adequate. That task seems to be falling to the state courts. For years, litigants have challenged state school funding formulas and the level of financing. The courts have tried to understand these school funding formulas in the context of their state constitutions and contemporary society. In the state of Washington, the supreme court ruled that "basic education means broad education opportunities needed in contemporary setting[s] to equip children for [their] role as citizens and competitors in [the] labor market and market place of ideas." Plus, "Legislature has [a] duty to define 'basic education' and make ample provision for its funding by means of regular and dependable tax sources and not special excise taxes."[11]

Note here the inclusion of labor market roles as consideration and the rejection of special excise taxes. Does this mean lottery monies would not be appropriate for funding schools? Since most broad-based taxes can be shown to be reasonably stable sources of funds, this exclusion of special excise taxes may refer to a special circumstance of consequence in Washington.

Subsequent to this ruling, the legislature directed the schools to support programs for workforce development. The Commission on Student Learning then set out goals for education, which included teaching "the importance of work and how performance and decisions directly affect future career and educational opportunities" and preparing students to "function as responsible individuals and contributing members of families, work groups, and communities."[12]

If workforce development is to be part of education, the schools must be well informed about future workforce requirements. This would, in turn, suggest that the states or the federal government provide the schools with such data. For decades, the U.S. Department of Labor and its affiliate organizations throughout the nation (variously known as employment security agencies, unemployment offices, or labor exchanges) have inadequately projected labor force requirements of the future.

These programs, at the state and federal levels, are orphans of

"Fellows I went to school with," Septum reflected, as Serina continued with her homework, "mostly went into the factories, if they came back home after the war. 'Course, some of 'em moved to other places, and some didn't come home at all."

"And the girls?" Serina asked, looking up from her book. "Oh, they stayed here. Lots of 'em. Maybe moved later." "Like Henna moved here?" Serina asked. "Yes, like Henna." He sighed and looked across to the distant garden.

operating agencies with other agendas. They are poorly funded and poorly supported by the data collection efforts of the states. In addition, with rapid changes in job classifications, education requirements, and technology, the task itself may be impossible.

Of great value might be efforts to identify the inadequacies of the existing labor force to do the jobs currently at hand. Then, education systems could assess their capabilities to participate in skill enhancement and training programs for those not currently in school, but holding jobs.

Politicians prefer, however, to seek employment for those on welfare, rather than to increase the productivity of the many more who are working below their capabilities. Moral outrage is the emotion brought to bear on the welfare issue. But could we not have a less passionate, but equally intense, concern for the foregone productivity of the millions who are among the inadequately educated members of the existing labor force?

The National Adult Literacy Survey (1992) found that "the majority of Americans saw little need to upgrade their current level of skills. Despite the fact that nearly half of all American adults scored at the two lowest of five levels of proficiency, nearly all American adults believed that they could read and write English well."[13]

———

"Tomfoolery," roared Septum. "What now?" Suzannah asked. "Business Week," he fumed, "same old stuff . . . 'With more and newer machines and equipment, U.S. workers would be more productive. And higher levels of investment would also enable companies to more quickly adopt new technologies.'* But they forget that new machines without workers who are capable of learning new ways is like a nice new race track where all the same old nags are running."

* (Business Week, July 8, 1996, 91)

School funding formulas are already complex, but they may not have the right elements in them. We have focused on the needs of children, on special education for children with learning disabilities. That is well and good. But we need to recognize the education requirements of the population, not just those of traditional school age. Tomorrow, when we think of education funding programs in light of the nation's need for increased income from its current working population, we should include factors related to the undereducated adult population.

The question remains, Do our current funding patterns for education distort the education we provide? If we need to educate those currently in the workforce, should we tax businesses as they do in Singapore, according to the number of workers they employ? This is a head tax and the same for those who earn low wages and for those in the upper brackets. This clearly discourages the employment of persons with low productivity.

Funds from this tax are available to businesses to train employees. Since your competitor is paying the tax and applying for training funds to upgrade his or her workers, you have an incentive to submit a better proposal and get those funds for your workers. Employers thus compete through a grant program for training monies.

The Singapore program is, as are many efforts in that remarkable and distinctive nation, stronger than the investment tax credit (ITC) proposals advanced for education in the U.S. The idea is to provide businesses with incentives for human capital development, comparable to the ITC of past years for physical capital. Monitoring such a program has its costs, but it would have the advantage, supporters contend, that individual businesses know best the skills needed by their workers.

It is possible to dream up new ways of spending on education without too much effort. The voucher plan, for example, which will be discussed in chapter 8, does not necessarily change the distribution of the financial burden of education. Vouchers, under almost every school choice program, would still be financed by traditional means.

New ways to finance education, however, require that we address some basic questions. Before we go any further, then, we will consider how the financial burden of education is distributed currently and how that might be altered.

"Rich people are not different from poor people," Sheldon said, although he knew Septum was listening to the radio broadcast of a baseball game.

Six

Who Should Pay?

My object all sublime,
I shall achieve in time,
To let the punishment fit the crime,
The punishment fit the crime.
—William S. Gilbert

Many economists will tell you that a good tax system is similar to the idealized judicial system of the Mikado. Taxes should be levied in a fashion consistent with the purposes of the function they support. What kind of function is education? How should it be supported?

The leading tax used to support primary and secondary public education in America has been the local property tax. It was a natural. What do we want a tax to do? The local property tax does it.

Most people feel taxes should be fair. By "fair" we mean two different things, which may be contradictory or ambiguous, but that does not stop us from wanting them. We believe that taxes should be related to income (or wealth) and to the benefits derived from government services. In addition, we believe that taxes should be easy to administer and reasonably stable as a revenue source.

Ability-to-pay

The first great principle of "fair" taxation says: Taxes should be based on ability-to-pay. We expect the rich to pay more than the poor. A proportional tax, which is a fixed percentage (today called a flat tax), does that job. With a 10% tax rate, a person earning $200,000 pays $20,000 in taxes. This is more than is paid by the person earning $50,000, whose taxes are $5,000.

Some people argue that 10% of a "rich" man's income does not deny, inconvenience, or hurt him as much as taking 10% from a "poor" man. This is the hypothesis of diminishing marginal utility of money, an idea widely disputed by people who have money. A progressive tax (with rates increasing as income rises) is based on this hypothesis.

Any truly flat tax, the same amount being collected from each person, is not in accord with the ability-to-pay principle. The head tax is a true flat tax. If you have a head, you pay a set sum, regardless of income.

The property tax meets the general expectation that a tax be based on an ability-to-pay principle. The more land you have, the larger your house, the better your neighborhood, the more likely you are to be a person of significant income. And the more you will pay in property taxes.

When land was truly a source of income, when many—if not most—people were farmers, the amount of land you owned was a good proxy for your income. Big fields, big herds of cattle represented wealth, the capitalized value of an income stream. The property tax was fair because it followed the ability-to-pay principle.

But today, the linkage between property and income is different. Henna Homestead may live in a large house on a big piece of land, yet be poor. Mrs. Homestead's property could reflect income of the past and have no relationship to her present or future income expectations. If she has high property taxes, they may be inconsistent with the ability-to-pay principle.

But Henna is not in the majority. For most Americans, their homes reflect both present and expected future income. Mortgages are made on that basis. The realtor and the mortgage company work from tables which indicate the price of a home consistent with the income expectations of the buying borrower. The property tax works in the sense that it links taxes with the ability to pay.

Yet, the property tax may be resented because it is seen as a tax on savings or a tax on consumption. If Mrs. Homestead has a property tax bill of $1,500 per year and $10,000 income, it might be argued that the tax rate is 15% on income. If she has $100,000 in equity in the home, the rate may be construed as a 1.5% tax on her invested capital. But holding her savings as capital in her home, unlike a bank or credit union account, unlike a mutual fund, does not yield a current flow of cash income. Where a bank account pays interest, her home only provides services.

A property tax, then, can be seen as a tax on the services rendered by a home. Henna Homestead lives in a house that could be rented for $600 per month ($7,200 per year). This is the imputed rental service she derives from living in the house. The annual property tax of $1,500 dollars is a 20.8% sales tax on those services. But why should housing services be taxed at a higher rate than the standard retail sales tax rate?

In today's world, where property is a consumer good for most of us and not a factor of production, as it is for agriculture and industry, the property tax may not be as "fair" as in the past.

Beneficiary taxation

The second principle of "fair" taxation calls for people to pay according to the value of the benefits they receive from the services provided. This is a private market concept applied to the public sector.

The principle dates back at least to the concepts of Locke and others in the 17th century who saw a world of individuals who contract for state services.[1] Under this philosophy, the rich again pay more taxes than the poor. With more to lose, the rich pay a higher fee for military, judicial, and police protection. As large land owners, the rich pay more for the roads which serve their larger properties. They pay more in taxes for roads also because they have more goods to move over the roads, and their carriages do more damage than the foot traffic of the poor.

The property tax is thus easily interpreted as a beneficiary tax. But when the property tax is used to

"Rich people are no different from poor people," Sheldon said, although he knew Septum was listening to the radio broadcast of a baseball game.

"Maybe not," Septum replied, without seeming to respond. "Fellow I know is nearly seven feet tall. Another fellow won't measure 5'5". Both of them play basketball. Taller fellow has an advantage even if the basket is the same for them both. Rich and poor folks may be the same, but they are different in what they can reach."

support education, the linkage begins to fray. Persons who do not have children in school are not primary beneficiaries of education services. We must believe in the externalities of education, in the reductions in crime and the advances of civilization, to accept taxes in support of education as a beneficiary tax. And are those benefits associated with the ownership of property?

In a purely individualistic mode, we could argue that parents are not the primary beneficiaries of education, unless we value the baby-sitting or custodial aspects of schooling at a high rate. Parents are usually considered beneficiaries because they are presumed to care about the welfare of their children. We would say that they derive current benefits in anticipation of the future well-being of their children. But what value do such benefits twenty years from now have for people who are willing to pay 18% and 21% credit card interest rates for the privilege of consuming goods and services today? Those who cannot forgo the goodies of the moment cannot be presumed to put much value in benefits so far in the future.

If the primary beneficiaries are to be taxed, then the students should pay for their education. We will return to that thought later.

In one sense, education spending does contribute to the welfare of the property tax payer. Although Henna Homestead does not have anyone from her household in the local schools, the value of her property itself may reflect the quality of education and the education facilities offered in her community. Since people with children do buy

"It's not fair," Serina whined, as she followed her mother into Henna's garden. "I don't take dessert, and I have to pay the same for lunch at school as those kids who have double banana splits."

"Injustice among the innocents," Henna Homestead smiled. "Henna," Suzannah rebuked, "it's not a joke. Our schools are run like socialist institutions. People should pay for what they use."

"And if you want to encourage the poor child to eat a full meal?" Henna asked. "But they're eating banana splits," Serina said, "and not just poor kids, but all kinds of kids."

"It's easy to solve that," Henna answered softly. "Make banana splits cost $2 each and charge nothing for spinach and Brussels sprouts. Then the rich will have dessert, and the poor will not go hungry."

homes, in part, on the basis of the schools serving that property, Henna's resale potential is a function of the services provided by schools. She may be said to realize the capitalized value of those services when she sells her home. This benefit, however, may be too tenuous to make her a strong supporter of increased taxes dedicated to education.

Ease of administration

Real property can be seen. Two neighbors can stand on the edge of a field and describe the property and come to agreement about its value. You and I could tour through a neighbor's home and begin to get some idea of its worth. Homes and fields do not move around on us. They stay put.

All of this makes the property tax easy to administer. It becomes more complex if we add specialized industrial machinery, home furnishings, and business inventories to the list of taxable property. It is less easy to determine the value of these items of "personal" property. Nor is it easy to identify what intangible assets a person or corporation may own. Stocks, bonds, and bank accounts are not something you can see and value while standing by the side of the field.

The retail sales tax has, over the years, become a comparatively easy tax to collect. Large retailers account for most of the sales in this country. They use cash registers to keep records and to check on the honesty of their employees. By applying the tax at the point of sale, state revenue departments can more readily audit receipts. Catalog and Internet sales are a different story. Taxes on these are notoriously difficult to collect since the revenue department in one state has limited means of determining the sales of merchants serving their citizens from other states.

The income tax is easiest to collect from wage and salary earners. Withholding of the individual's estimated tax liability on a current basis is a superb means of collecting taxes. And the employer gets to use the money withheld every week until it is due at the Internal Revenue Service a month after the close of the quarter.

As more and more professionals and independent business people follow standard bookkeeping procedures, it is possible to audit their receipts. But in the world of the backyard mechanic, the drug dealer, and the furnace repairman, income flows are difficult to substantiate.

Taxes on other forms of income have become more readily available as uniform booking and computer technology have advanced. Dividends and interest payments are keyed to an individual's social security number. But the $55 a week Henna Homestead gets from a college student for the back bedroom may go unrecorded.

The property tax can be collected locally. That was one of its advantages in the past. But the sales and income taxes are more difficult to collect locally. For example, which jurisdiction has the right to tax my income if I live in New Jersey and work in New York? To which government should I pay the sales tax if I shop in Chicago and live in Milwaukee? Are we taxpayers where we live or where our economic activity takes place? The modern world is messy.

Revenue stability

The property tax is a fairly stable tax. Year after year, it can be depended on to yield about the same amount of revenue for government.

If times are good, total receipts rise because new properties are added to the tax rolls. With good sales, the shoe store builds another unit across town. When times are bad, the shoe store may close its cross-town store, but the building remains. And local governments do not reassess often enough to reflect the downturn in receipts on a vacant property.

It is the sluggishness of assessment practices that makes the property tax a stable revenue source. Retail sales taxes and income taxes are much more sensitive to changes in economic performance. In good times, sales and income tax receipts rise with the economy. In bad times, income taxes fall more than sales tax receipts because people spend out of savings.

Education expenditures, however, are not related to short-term economic fluctuations. They move with the general level of prices and, even more so, with the changes in the student population. But these are generally long-term variations. Price changes are not easy to anticipate, but enrollment projections are quite feasible, particularly at the state level. At the school district level, enrollment projections may be difficult when there is robust building activity, the closing of a military base, or a layoff at a major factory.

The ideal tax

"What is the best way to finance education?" Given the diverse objectives we have for education and the complex nature of education's role in our society, that answer is simple. The best way to finance education is through a complex arrangement of taxes and fees.

But we already have that, you will protest. Right, and what is wrong with complexity, if it does what we want? The problem we have today is that our current system does not do what we want.

We want a school financing formula that reflects the two basic principles of taxation: those who benefit pay, and those who pay contribute according to their means.

A deferred federal income tax would do the job. First, students would pay when they received market rewards for their labor services. Virtually every study of the subject shows that increments to education result in income gains for the individual. We cannot say which part of income is attributable to education; hence, we need

"What good did my schooling do?" Suzannah asked Henna, as they sat shelling peas. *"Sheldon is an accountant, so it's obvious his income is a result of what he learned in school or later on the job. There is nothing instinctive about accounting."*

"And what you do is all instinct?" Henna commented, not waiting for a reply. *"Your ability to function in society is enhanced by your education. The problem is we don't know how much because we do not have good measures of functioning in society. Some of what you know as a mother, a wife, a consumer, a voter, a driver, a citizen is also the result of what you learned in school, and some is due to what we learn on the job—by living.*

"But you probably are more effective because of your schooling than you would be without it."

"That's comforting," Suzannah said. *"Yes, but not convincing,"* Henna added, reading the younger woman's mind.

not differentiate between the wages of the first and last hour of the day. The more income the student earns as a worker, the more he or she pays in taxes.

Second, other citizens will also pay at a time when those former students are active members of society, since those students' "improved behaviors," resulting from their education, will generate positive externalities.

But what if a person does not enter the labor market? How will that person's education be repaid under a deferred income tax scheme?

The answer: it won't be repaid, at least, not directly. Those who choose not to join the labor force will escape paying back for their education. However, to the extent that these persons are parents or caregivers, we anticipate that their education will contribute to the improved quality of life for the next or the preceding generation. But whatever they chose to do, would they, and we, be better off if they were less educated?

Some beneficiaries of education, by their choice of a lifestyle, can escape taxation and repayment. Yes, some will become beach bums, inarticulate poets, perennial advocates for lost causes, and persistent business failures. But do many choose to be inarticulate or unsuccessful?

However, many people do choose careers that do not maximize their monetary income. They become teachers or members of the clergy. Their choices reduce tax revenues. Yet, this is clearly not a misallocation of education resources. Our hope is to provide education that permits individuals to make enlightened choices about the direction of their lives.

We would not want a financing scheme that distorts utilization of the education system. Specifically, we do not want students either under- or over-utilizing education resources. But, primary and secondary education is not a service that one is likely to "over-consume." It is hard to imagine Serina becoming a perpetual high school student or being continuously enrolled in college as a means of avoiding adult responsibilities.

Certainly, the market potential of each person will not be realized. Some persons will become disabled, some will die without paying back their education expenditures. We recognize that not every seed planted blossoms as a marketable commodity. Our hope is to reduce the "waste" of education; but we cannot deny opportunities to those who will not be "harvested" as we might wish.

The second aspect of the proposed tax plan involves the externalities of education, that is, the extent to which my income is a function of the education of my co-workers in society. A federal income tax on me captures some of the benefits I realize from the education of others. Imperfect, yes. But enforceable, and without the imperfections of taxing property, retail sales, and income in a jurisdiction that is not likely to be where the benefits of education are realized.

The idea of a deferred federal income tax is to have each generation pay for its own education, albeit after that education is provided. It need not be a strict accounting with carefully maintained records of how much of society's resources were expended on each student, although that is technically feasible in today's world.

Financing education through a deferred income tax is congruent with today's thinking. Beneficiary taxation and market orientation have captured the public imagination, as much as the public thinks of such matters. Taken a step further, if the funds expended today on the granddaughter of Septum Sixpack were to be considered a loan, little Serina Seriatim would be expected to repay those funds from future earnings.

This may sound far-fetched, but it requires only that the student loan programs for college education be extended to earlier grades. We would teach children to write their names the first week of kindergarten so that they could sign their loan notes. A pure beneficiary tax in support of education would extend credit to students, with repayment linked to their future income. With today's computer resources, this need not be a national program.

Little Serina would have an account against which her education charges would be levied. If she studied finger painting, the costs would be entered, with allowance for overhead, just as in hospital cost accounting. If she chose something less costly, let us say a program of meditation, she would incur less debt.

How does the government finance this student borrowing? It could use current taxes levied on her grandfather, her parents, and all other Americans. They would receive credits in their accounts and earn interest, all payable in the future by Serina. In effect, Serina borrows from older generations through a program of taxation. The student incurs the debt and is obligated to repay from income, if income is available. An annual bill is sent to the student, now income-earner, and the borrowed money is repaid, with interest or some adjustment for cost-of-living or increase in average wage levels. This billing could be more frequent and even a form of withholding, to reduce its visibility.

Alternatively, the government could raise funds in the private market, borrowing from the public and repaying from the deferred income tax. This has the advantage that the funds provided for education are given voluntarily, rather than through compulsory taxation. Here, savers choose to finance education. Coercion is not a factor, although extensive bond drives, as in wartime, might be necessary.

School borrowing

Thus far, we have assumed that the government, presumably the federal government, is financing Serina's education. But these devices could be used at the local level. The problem at this level is creating a mechanism that follows Serina as she moves from employer to employer, district to district, state to state, through marriage, divorce, and a whimsical name change to match her emerging personality.

Instead of borrowing in the name of a student, individual schools or school corporations could borrow in the bond market in their own names. Already, school districts borrow for capital projects with the bonds secured by future taxes. Here, they would borrow for current operations with the income of a cohort or class of students offered as security.

Economists describe education as the primary means of forming human capital. Therefore, it seems reasonable to pay for capital formation through voluntary private sector savings. Serina and her classmates would be obligated to repay the school, which would retire the bonds. No government need stand behind these bonds, even though the risk factor on them would appear high.

Schools serving low-income children, or more specifically, schools serving children for whom the bond market has low expectations of future income, would have difficulty floating bonds without paying very high interest rates. This might give rise to government subsidies or guarantees.

Such debentures could be packaged as home mortgages are in today's market. They could be sold as investments to pension funds and other long-term investors. However, until the courts recognize the legality of obligating the future income of children, there would be few investors willing to buy such notes. But parents, grandparents, churches, or even governments could provide guarantees of repayment and/or subsidize interest payments. After enough years, each school would have a reputation, a credit rating, for its ability to produce students who repay their bonds.

This approach has many of the drawbacks of privatizing education. But it would be a way for determined parents with low incomes and insignificant marketable assets to finance enclave schools. Here, children who are particularly well-motivated could be provided with education based on their potential, rather than the pocketbooks of their parents. As a supplement to education financing, it has some appeal.

Some might argue that none of these proposals has even a moderate chance of being adopted. Why bother bringing them forth? Because they meet our principles of beneficiary and ability-to-pay financing. Because they illustrate ways to shift the burden of financing education from the current generation to future beneficiaries, which is consistent with our desire to relieve the current generation of responsibility for education and our recognition of that traditional responsibility. And because . . . once-strange ideas have been known to become part of conventional wisdom with the passage of time.

An immodest proposal

Traditionally, parents and grandparents develop the skills of their little ones. The implied social contract was that the little ones would then support their elders. But today, little Serina is taught by grandfather Septum, father Sheldon, and mother Suzannah so that she can survive and prosper in the world she has to face.

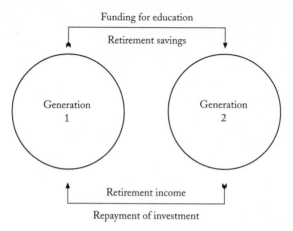

Figure 6.1 Intergenerational Support

Our era has smaller, less-connected families. Older people pay for the education of younger people to whom they are not related, except by sharing space in the same geo-political entity. At the same time, workers pay for the retirement and health care of older citizens through taxation, and provide for their own retirement through various forms of savings.

Why not merge our desire for beneficiary taxation with our need for retirement income? We can use funds that are saved by one generation to finance the education of the next. Then, retirement income can flow from the earnings generated by that education, as in *Figure 6.1.* This means we would stop the current deceptive practice of using our social security taxes to fund the nation's annual deficit. The social security trust fund would be used to finance education. Future taxes on income would then be used to provide retirement income.

This approach helps to restructure education finance. We can move away from local financing of schools. Everywhere in America, young people would have equal financial underpinnings to their education. Children in poor districts would not be handicapped by the income of their parents and neighbors, *if the level of federal support is adequate.* But there should be no limitations or penalties on districts that choose to supplement the resources of their schools. The goal of basic or foundation support is to cover the requirements of a sound education in the context of our times. It is not intended to equalize resources across boundaries by suppressing the wealthy or the dedicated from making additional efforts.

It is easy to argue that the property tax is not appropriate for financing education. The benefits of education accrue to individuals, independent of their property ownership. These benefits may not be realized until far in the future and, often, at considerable distance from the point of taxation.

Our discussion of migration will indicate one national aspect of education. In addition, the need to satisfy the claims of a growing older population on income also implies a national interest in education. Together, these factors suggest the need for federal rather than state or local funding of public primary and secondary education. Federal funds could be used to replace the property tax and to provide an appropriate level of spending for every public school child in the nation.

However, since the states do not all rely on property taxation for a common share of public education finance, we cannot guarantee the end of property taxation for public schools. Those decisions must rest with the individual states. Federal support would be geared to meet a major share of the equalization and foundation finance programs of the states.

The goal of the states should be to move education finance away from local taxes. States that have already advanced in that direction should not be penalized for their prior progress. A formula for the distribution of federal funds would have to be based on the support of education, not the type of taxes currently used for that purpose.

How is the federal government to finance education? And, what portion of education? We argue for federal financing of education because students are mobile, and those who share in the earnings workers generate are scattered over the entire nation. It follows that we would not support federal financing of buildings which are not mobile. (See chapter 8 for additional comments on other expenditures currently made by schools that are not appropriate, in my view, for either federal or state support.)

Five new tax sources, using 1992 data, would raise a total of $101.6 billion dollars. (See *Figure 6.2.*) New taxes will not be readily supported by the elected representatives of the American people. But if these federal funds can replace other tax burdens, it is worth exploring the possibilities.

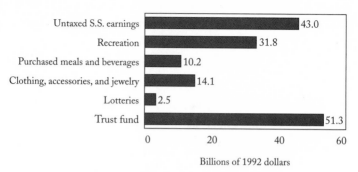

Figure 6.2 Proposed Federal Sources to Fund Education
Total: $152.9 billion

In school year 1992, local governments raised $104.1 billion for public elementary and secondary education.[2] Since a significant portion of this amount went to debt retirement and interest payments, which I presume federal funds would not support, the $101.6 billion in new federal taxes in 1992 would have adequately replaced local spending on education services.

Untaxed earnings

For the year 1992, the Social Security Administration estimated that 12.8% of total earnings ($384 billion) was beyond the taxable limit. Although that maximum level rises each year, the percent beyond the limit is not necessarily reduced. If the 11.2% tax rate for Old Age and Survivors Insurance had been applied to this amount, it would have generated $43 billion.[3] The social security tax is a flat tax consistent with many of the proposals placed before the Congress. It has a single rate. It applies only to wage and salary income and does not include capital gains, dividends, interest, or rent. Eliminating the cap would make it a less regressive tax.

Recreation

In 1992, Americans spent $318 billion on recreation. A 10% tax on all forms of recreation spending would have raised nearly $32 billion.[4] As shown earlier (in *Figure 1.1*), this category of personal consumption has been rising at an 8.6% annual rate while all personal consumption expenditures have managed a 7.4% growth rate. How many fewer video rentals would we expect if rates rose from $3 to $3.30? Would rock or symphony concerts that currently sell tickets at $20 have many more empty seats with $22 tickets?

Meals and beverages for consumption away from home
A 5% tax on these items would have raised approximately $10 billion in 1992.[5] Eating out is a growing aspect of American culture. It is a great convenience after a day of work. It is also part of an affluent lifestyle and is probably more readily taxed than many other forms of consumption.

Clothing, accessories, and jewelry
If taxed at a 5% rate, these consumer goods would have yielded approximately $14 billion in 1992.[6] How many pairs of shoes do you own? How many ties does the American businessman possess? Have higher prices diminished the sale of athletic shoes?

Lotteries
A 10% tax on lotteries in 1992 would have produced over $2.5 billion in revenues. This tax is not essential to our argument. Most Americans probably could support added taxes on marginal discretionary spending. In addition, it would be desirable to increase taxes on all forms of gambling and channel those funds to education. If we wish to teach our children that the rewards in life are based on productivity and not chance, let those who think (or hope) differently pay for that lesson.

"Why should the government be taxing fun?" Septum asked me, after I had put forth my ideas on public finance. "Wouldn't we be better off taxing sin? Why take good things away from people? Won't that just cut down the incentive to work, if you can't enjoy the money you earn?"

"I don't think that Americans will give up fun because we tax it," I answered. "I am depending on their seemingly inexhaustible demand for fun, for thrills, for sensation to keep the money flowing. Taxing sin (like alcohol, cigarettes, and other evils) is great, but sin taxes can be used to offset the adverse effects of using those goods.

"The things I want to tax (other than gambling) have no adverse effects. They are the extras in life on which we can draw for funds to keep our society productive."

"Seems to me," he responded, "you're just a spoilsport. Bet you didn't dance at your prom." As usual, Septum was right; I didn't go to my prom.

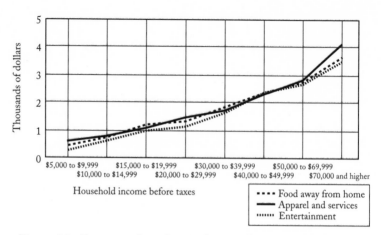

Figure 6.3 Consumer Spending by Income Bracket, 1992-93

With the exception of removing the cap on social security, the argument will be raised that each of these taxes will have adverse consequences for the poor. But to support that contention, one would have to show that these taxes are more regressive than the taxes they would replace. *Figure 6.3* shows that all of these expenditures rise as income rises. But the portion of income spent on these items tends to fall as income rises (See *Figure 6.4*.)[7] Note, however, that the categories in these two graphs are not identical to those discussed earlier. Entertainment is but a subset of recreation. It excludes some of the capital goods which are part of recreation spending. These data would require reconciliation before any conclusive statement could be made about the progressive-regressive aspect of the taxes proposed here.

The taxes on recreation, eating out, clothing, accessories and jewelry, plus the lotteries may be interpreted as a Calvinistic plot to reform sinful America. The issue at hand, if we need to be reminded, is a massive reorientation of the economy in the near term.

Many argue that Americans need to reduce consumption and increase investment. That is precisely what this program is designed to achieve. If future spending is reduced on those expenditure categories targeted for higher taxes, and the taxes collected are channeled into the formation of

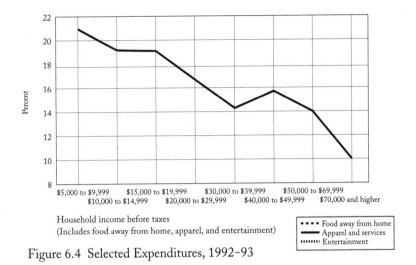

Figure 6.4 Selected Expenditures, 1992-93

human capital, we will have seen what we want—less consumption and more investment.

The final and largest part of the new sources for federal support of education does not require any new tax. This would be the redirection of the annual net flow into the social security trust fund. Instead of spending those funds—$51.3 billion in 1992—on the various programs which contribute to the federal deficit, they would be earmarked for education.

Of course, the problem foreseen is the decline of this surplus and its shift to a negative position in the years ahead. But that is what this proposal is intended to alleviate, if not forestall. If those sums could be used to augment the education of high school students and those adults who have weak workforce skills, we might see the productivity gains needed to avert the anticipated crisis in the social security trust funds.

How will the money be spent? Will federal funding mean federal control? Does all this result in a powerful U.S. Department of Education? Those issues are about to be addressed.

"When a child walks to school, she becomes part of the community," Septum explained.

Seven

Who Should Run the Schools?

Some girls can bake a pie
made up of prunes and quinces,
Some make an oyster fry,
others are good at blintzes.
Some lovely girls have done
wonders with turkey stuffin'
But I have found the one
who can really make corn muffins.

—Ira Gershwin

America has seen a continuing decrease in the number of school districts and corporations in the U.S. While that number exceeded 119,000 in 1938, it dwindled to fewer than 15,000 in 1994. However, this massive consolidation, an economic and social phenomenon of great consequence, is now being questioned by many would-be reformers.

Consolidation took place as we tried to save money and improve the quality of education simultaneously. We thought we could improve the efficiency of education (save money) through economies of scale. Bigger units, the story went, could reduce duplication, take advantage of quantity discounts, develop specialized resources, and broaden the curriculum. Small units could never afford such diversity.

Bigger units often meant building modern new schools (always good for the architects, consulting engineers, bond lawyers, and other parasites of the education industry). These were frequently located with care at some point of no consequence, someplace on neutral ground. That way, the units brought together would not suffer the pain of being enveloped by each other. They could both surrender their identities to the new nonentity.

This process of consolidation, opponents told us, would destroy community identity, eradicate valuable traditions, reduce property values, and harm the environment. It was a policy designed to enrich school bus manufacturers and drivers. Democratic values were being endangered, parental control would be reduced, and we would all rue the day.

"When a child walks to school," Septum whispered to Serina, "she becomes part of the community. She learns who lives where. And those who live along her path come to know her. She memorizes each crack in the sidewalk and the circumference of each tree. The seasons have reality; weather is felt in the bones rather than seen through a window."

"Father," Suzannah called from inside the house, "stop filling that child's head with the romanticism of a poorly recalled past."

"And," Septum lowered his voice, "children enjoy liberties when they walk that they can never have on a school bus. Candy stores and excursions to forbidden places, secret luxuries and unsavory tales of adult life are passed along from child to child, keeping alive the traditions of childhood."

"Yes," Suzannah added, now appearing on the porch unexpectedly, "and beatings by bullies, assaults by perverts, and who knows what else. Oh, Father, please let my daughter live in her world, and don't make her long for yours."

Everyone was right. All those good and all those terrible things happened. States encouraged, and often required, consolidation because reason and available evidence discounted the ability of smaller schools to provide efficient education at that time.

Now, with new and significant technology available for education, including two-way television, the Internet, and specialized instructional materials, there is a reexamination of the ideas behind consolidation and a movement for a return to smaller units.

Before continuing, let's consider the local school district. What powers does it have? What powers should it have? In today's world, is there a more presumptuous, overrated education organization than the local school corporation or district? Is there a form of government more revered as the model of democracy, the last defense against Big Brother and thought control?

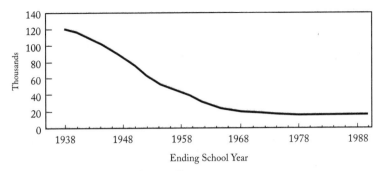

Figure 7.1 U.S. Public School Districts

Local school districts

Local schools are creatures of the states. The school boards and the local schools, which many politicians extol, do not exist as significant policy-making organizations, except in the collective imagination of our nation.

Perhaps it should be otherwise, but state departments of education direct what is taught and who teaches. Often, states will dictate how many minutes per day are to be allocated to specific functions or tasks. Micromanagement reigns supreme in our schools. Teachers often feel that they are automatons programmed by the legislature and the state school agency. This pattern for operating our schools has existed and been reinforced by the courts year after year.

Parents, teachers, administrators, children, and employers may think the schools exist for their purposes. But that is true only when such purposes are in harmony with the interests of the state. This was made clear by the supreme court of Tennessee in 1899, when it declared the following:

> It is said the schools do not belong to the state, but to the people, and while, in a certain sense, this is true, it is, at least, but a play on words. The system is inaugurated, operated, shaped, supported, and controlled by the state through its legislature, but for the benefit of the people, and as in all other

matters of public concern, the people act through their immediate representatives, the legislature.

[The] object of the public school system is to prevent crime, by educating the people, and thus, by providing and securing a higher state of intelligence and morals, conserve the peace, good order, and well being of society.[1]

Local schools in America exist to further the aims of the state. You may not like it, and I am not suggesting this is how it should be. But this is how it is, even in New Hampshire, where, in 1912, the supreme court found that "while most people regard the public schools as a means of great personal advantage to pupils, the fact is too often overlooked that they are governmental means of protecting the state from the consequences of an ignorant and incompetent citizenship."[2]

The schools do not exist to relieve parents of the burdens or responsibilities of education. They are not intended to be a means of redistributing income, if the Illinois supreme court is to be believed:

The public school system of the State was not established and has not been maintained as a charity or from philanthropic motives.

The conduct and maintenance of schools by school directors, school trustees and boards . . . however beneficial to individuals, are not undertaken from philanthropic or charitable motives, but for the protection, safety, and welfare of the citizens of the state in the interest of good government.[3]

These views are based on ideas current at the beginning of our republic. The Northwest Ordinance of 1787, which led to the formation of Ohio, Michigan, Indiana, Illinois, Wisconsin, and Minnesota, declared that "religion, morality and knowledge being necessary to good government and the happiness of mankind, schools and the means of educations shall forever be encouraged."[4]

This argument, in its extreme form, says the schools exist to prevent social disorder. Reading, writing, arithmetic are substitutes for cattle prods, fire hoses, and martial law. Anxiety over the behavior of other people's children was, and continues to be, the great stimulus to public education.

The nobler sentiments of enlightenment and receptivity to the finer aspects of civilization have been the sugar coating of professional educators and liberal moralists. The concept of education as the path to income enhancement and the development of a more suitable workforce are the inventions of economists and Chambers of Commerce. Schooling, according to the doctrine presented in these legal findings, is but society's pre-emptive strike against prospective mayhem.

Thus, the school board exists as the state's agent in a locality. All powers that the local board may have are derived from those of the state. The states have authority over education because this important function is not mentioned in the Constitution of the United States. Amendment X of the Bill of Rights grants to the states those "powers not delegated to the United States by the Constitution."

By default or by intent, the federal government was given no role in education. Although education is an important part of the Northwest Ordinance of 1787, the Constitution and the Federalist Papers are silent on the subject. Over the years, amendments to the Constitution regarding education have been associated with the teaching or practice of religion. As today, there have been efforts in the past to get more religion into schools. But it appears that no one has sponsored a constitutional amendment to ensure that education is a major function of the government of the United States. Is this an idea whose time has come?

The U.S. Department of Education, which many would abolish, exists without explicit constitutional authority. The federal government's role in education is defended on the basis of the phrase "promote the general welfare," which appears in the Preamble to the Constitution. It might as well be based on the remaining phrases, "insure domestic tranquility, provide for the common defense . . . and secure the blessings of liberty to ourselves and our posterity. . . ."

Local school boards can choose the school colors. They have limited curriculum and textbook choices. They make decisions on capital expenditures. They decide if and where to build what kind of school. Thus, they are important to architects, real estate developers, and attorneys who act as bond counsel. Their capital investment decisions, however, are often passive. Developers build the homes, and the schools must trail after them.

Enrollments decline in neighborhoods that once thrived, and schools must be closed or converted to other uses. School boards are powerful, but not in control of events, and they act alone.

Enrollments may be burgeoning in a suburban area that is artificially divided into two or more school districts. Instead of optimizing enrollments throughout the area and building just one new unit, we may find several or no new schools being built. As long as school districts are not seen as administrative units of the state and, instead, are viewed as bastions of individualism, inefficient solutions will abound.

The abilities of school districts to direct curriculum, establish qualifications for teachers, raise taxes, and issue bonds are controlled in full or in part by their state legislatures. School attendance districts may be under local control, if no desegregation ruling has placed this authority in the hands of the courts. The length of skirts worn by cheerleaders is still within the domain of most local boards.

And why should schooling be controlled locally? Conventional political dogma states that schools should be controlled by parents because they have the interests of their children at heart. Parents, it is argued, know what is best for their children.

But the history of education in America demonstrates that we have

"Why don't you run for the school board?" Sheldon suggested to Suzannah. He was reading the newspaper while she bemoaned the state of public education.

"I don't have the time, and what do I know about schools?" she answered. "You know as much as the people who are there now," he said with unaccustomed warmth and sincerity.

"But there's so much bureaucracy and legalism! An ordinary person is bound to be buffaloed by administrators, the union, attorneys, and the rest," she responded. "And most important, I don't need the hassle of neighbors who want a new swimming pool calling at all hours of the day to object because I think the priorities are a school library with books.

"Why don't you run?" she asked, returning the ball to his side of the net. "Me?" he laughed. "I couldn't put up with the pettiness, the jingoism, the egotism, and the selfishness of concerned citizens."

"Oh," she sneered. "I'd think you'd be right at home."

It was several hours before they talked again.

not, at all times and in all places, shared this happy, perhaps naive, view. Compulsory attendance and universal education were supported because it was argued that parents themselves were not good citizens and were unfit mentors for their children. These patrician views still exist, although no politician would voice them today.

It would make sense to have local schools run by local people — if they were providing education for the citizens of the community — the future parents, voters, and workers of that town. But we do not live in that world. Maybe once upon a time, when the nation was young, we did live in such places. But no longer. Ours is a nation of people in motion.

A national agenda

In 1990, only 61.8% of the population were Americans living in the state in which they were born. This means 38.2% of the residents of this country had been born somewhere other than the state in which they were residing. We do not know when they moved. But clearly, many of them were prepared for life in schools governed by states different from the one where they later lived and worked. Education standards thought to be appropriate in their home areas were embodied in people later resident all over America.

Let's forget about persons born outside the U.S. and look only at native-born Americans. These persons numbered 225.7 million at the last census in 1990; that was 90.7% of the total U.S. population. Human capital moves easily across borders within the nation, and people carry their education with them as an asset or a liability.

Of these 225.7 million native-born Americans, 72 million (31.9%) lived outside the state in which they were born. At some time before 1990, each of these persons had been a domestic migrant. The education system in their states of birth, presumably, tried to provide a course of study which suited them for their lives in those states. But was it appropriate for the states where they finally settled?

Figure 7.2 tells the story from the point of view of the receiving states, the story of in-migration. Eight states in 1990 had 50% or more of their

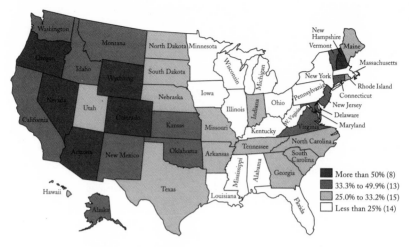

Figure 7.2 Percent of 1990 Population
Born in Another State

U.S.-born population coming from outside that state. Nevada, which led the nation in this dubious distinction, had nearly 76% of its U.S.-born population as in-migrants from other states. In 13 states, U.S.-born in-migrants accounted for one-third to one-half of the population. Only Louisiana (18.9%), Pennsylvania (16.4%), and New York (16.3%) had fewer than one in five U.S.-born persons coming from out of state.

Figure 7.3 examines America's domestic migration from the viewpoint of the states exporting human capital. Three states had more than half of their sons and daughters living outside their borders in 1990: Montana (56.7%), North Dakota (56%), and South Dakota (52.7%). Obviously, the charm of the northern plains may be less than the tourist agencies of those states proclaim. Another 25 states had between one-third and one-half of their children living elsewhere in 1990. Only two states (Texas at 21% and California at 19.5%) had less than 25% of their native born persons residing in another state in 1990.[5]

How can we expect uncoordinated state programs to provide our citizens with the education needed in our times of shifting populations?

One of the reasons for the common school in the 19th century was to meet the perceived threats of cultural diversity. Today, states with heavy

Tightrope to Tomorrow

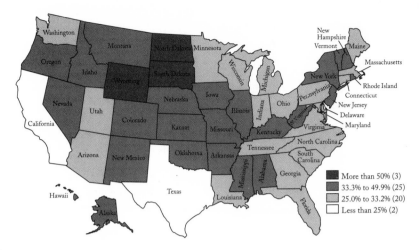

Figure 7.3 Percent of Population Living
outside State of Birth in 1990

in-migration must assimilate populations educated under a wide variety
of standards. What is the common imagery of a people who have no
standard education background? As TV and the Internet offer ever wider
ranges of entertainment choices and experiences, only the schools are left
to provide citizens with a common cultural, philosophical, and political
heritage.

Employers in the labor-importing states cannot depend on the education systems of the labor-exporting states to provide a consistent level
of knowledge or capability to learn. In a nation which supports, encour-
ages, and glorifies the free mobility of the population, we risk significant
costs associated with that movement.

If we did not have significant mobility of labor, corporations might
build and operate their own secondary schools. A company with a major
facility in a given town would have an incentive to organize a school that
would feed workers to its plant.

This would be an extension of vertical integration. Control by the
company would be extended backward on to the supply of labor.[6] Students
would be focused on skills and subjects that the company deemed appropriate for future employment.

The idea has some appeal. In a modified form, it is being pushed by business groups all over the United States. However, many corporate leaders believe our schools should provide students with skills that make them less costly to hire. They wish to have training at public expense rather than provide training on the job.

What kind of curriculum would please the business community? Would American literature and more than a smattering of history be required in such schools? Some education reformers are willing to say that the employer is the ultimate consumer of public education services. This approach denies those components of education that are not related to production but are integral to the life of the student as a consumer. It is a confusion between the role of schools as places offering training *and* education and as places offering *only* training.

But students are mobile, and employers will not invest heavily in resources they cannot control. To increase their own mobility, large corporations, in particular, have an interest in improving the quality of education everywhere, which, in turn, improves the quality of labor in all jurisdictions.

The logical conclusion would be a national call for significant, widely adopted standards of education. But the rhetoric of our times opposes most efforts supporting national standards. Rather, the rapid reformers would move more control to localities, to local school boards, to individual schools. Imagine the potential chaotic educational outputs of such a system. Already our education system yields inadequate qualities. No imagination is necessary to understand how a few school districts might excel while most would be overwhelmed by mediocrity.

This picture of migration becomes more serious when we consider localities. Let's look at the amount of population mobility in just one state: Indiana. The Hoosier state is fairly typical in terms of out-migration. As noted earlier, nationally, 68.1% of U.S.-born Americans

"Learning," Septum said, delivering a lecture for my benefit, "includes education and training."

"The difference being . . ." I left the field to him. "Education prepares you for life while training helps you earn a living," he said.

"Sententious wisdom," I said. "No extra charge," he replied.

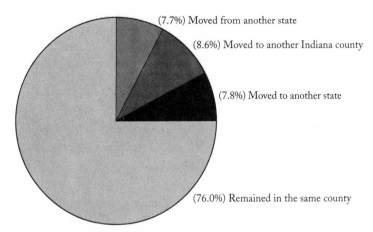

(7.7%) Moved from another state

(8.6%) Moved to another Indiana county

(7.8%) Moved to another state

(76.0%) Remained in the same county

Figure 7.4 Migration of Indiana Population
1985 to 1990

were living in their state of birth in 1990. The figure for Indiana was 68.4%, with only South Carolina (at 68.2%) closer to the national percentage.

But with local control of schools, we would want to consider the out-migration from each school corporation. The Census data do not support such an inquiry. We can get closer to that analysis, however, by considering county level information from the 1990 Census.

The Census asks people to indicate where they lived five years earlier. In 1990, Indiana had 5.15 million persons age 5 and older. Of these, 434,000 had moved to Indiana between 1985 and 1990. During those same years, based on the Census in other states, there were nearly as many 1985 Hoosiers living in other states in 1990 (431,000). Hence, 865,000 persons were involved in a nationwide exchange of human capital, when we look at just this one state, over just a single five-year period.

But there is more to migration than just crossing a state line. In 1990, there were 477,000 persons living in an Indiana county different from their Indiana county of residence in 1985. In sum, more than 1.34 million persons moved into or out of Indiana counties in just five years.[7] When we consider all persons who were Hoosiers, either in 1985 or 1990, we find that nearly one-quarter of them were migrants. (See *Figure 7.4*.)

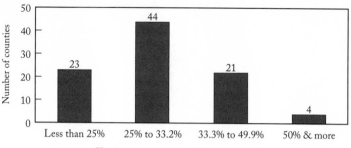

Figure 7.5 Migration in Indiana Counties
1985 to 1990

To get some idea of what this means, let's compare the number of Indiana migrants (people entering or leaving a county) to the number of non-migrants (people who did not move across a county line) between '85 and '90. For Indiana as a whole, that number was equal to 31.7%, nearly one-third of which was resident in the same county in both 1985 and 1990.

Of Indiana's 92 counties, 69 had the total number of migrants crossing county lines exceed 25% of the total number remaining within the same county. And this was just in a five-year period. (See *Figure 7.5*.) Everywhere, even in stolid Indiana, employers concerned about local schools should also recognize this extensive migration and its implications for workforce development programs.

We have no knowledge of how many persons live out their lives in the school districts where they receive their educations. We may suspect that it has been a decreasing number as the decades progressed through this century. Anecdotal evidence says that high school reunions are difficult to assemble because so many graduates move.

Yet, rigid advocates for local schools would apply local values and local standards for the education of a population that will be highly mobile, and which must meet international competitive circumstances. Is it going too far to call such views "presumptuous"?

TIGHTROPE TO TOMORROW

A middle-ground proposal

Education is a function of the states that would be well served by federal financing. Yet, the very idea of federal financing causes hands to shake and eyes to twitch if it is mentioned with any seriousness. Fears immediately surface that federal bureaucrats will impose inappropriate standards. Fear mongers of the political extremes sense a plot to control the minds of youth and infiltrate alien ideologies into the curriculum.

Also, the organization which might administer a federal funding program is widely distrusted. The U.S. Department of Education is viewed as unnecessary at best and un-American at worst by its critics. Its defenders, if any, are few and not particularly vocal.

But if federal funds are to be used in support of education, it makes sense to have criteria for that distribution. Those criteria need to be set in line with the national objectives for the education system. Ideally, they would be in terms of performance, while recognizing differences in the education impediments faced by different states, school districts, and individual schools.

When the nation's economy was subject to violent contractions because of a volatile banking environment, it established the Federal Reserve System. We suffered through a series of "panics," inflationary expansions and depressions. The business cycle was taken to be a natural phenomenon.

But in recent years, under the leadership of Paul Volker and Alan Greenspan, the Fed has gained respect and acclaim for its performance.[8] Is a comparable organization a feasible mechanism for distributing federal support for public education?

A Federal (or National) Education Commission might be similar to the Federal Reserve in some ways. It would distribute federal funds in support of education, and it would set criteria for the distribution of such funds. The U.S. Department of Education could continue to collect data and to administer other programs, but it would not be involved in setting the policies of the Commission.

Just as the U.S. government has both the Department of the Treasury and the Federal Reserve System operating in the financial sector, the Education Department and the Commission would exist side by side. At times, the Treasury and the Fed are not in harmony. Political considerations, at times, have weighed heavily in the views at the Treasury.

But unlike it, the structure of the Commission could be insulated from politics. It could have a board made up of representatives elected by regional bodies composed of state superintendents of public instruction (or their counterparts). They would serve staggered terms. The Chair could be appointed by the President, with the usual advice and consent of the Congress, and might serve no more than two five-year terms.

It would be counterproductive to set out the specifics of such an organization as it is the detail which often attracts detractors. The main function of the Commission would be to set criteria for the distribution of federal funds. Those funds would be drawn from the Social Security Trust Fund, augmented by lifting the cap on eligible income. They would also include monies from taxes earmarked by Congress for distribution by the Commission, as discussed in chapter 6. To avoid annual political tampering with the flow of funds, taxes designated for the Commission's distribution would have to be exempt from the usual machinations of the Congress. Rates would have to be established and set for a given number of years, beyond the current budget cycle. Funds could not be withheld from distribution (as is the current practice with the transportation trust funds).

There is no guarantee that such a Commission would constitute a body of superior wisdom. It would be based on the same principles, however, that stimulated the Founding Fathers in establishing representative democracy in America. Membership would be geographically balanced, and members would not be elected directly by the people, but drawn, instead, from groups of persons (elected or appointed) who have been chosen for particular qualities in their own states.

Such a commission, made up of state representatives, is most unlikely to preempt the powers of the states. This would continue our tradition of keeping educational decision making in the State House and out of Washington. But the states would have to agree on a formula for the distribution of funds. The allocations would have to recognize the diversity of conditions that exist across the nation and still be consistent with national goals.

A National Commission would get attention from the national press. It would be subjected to more effective examination of education policy issues than are the decisions made by state legislatures. National lobbying groups would give the Commission much to consider.

To the extent that federal funds substitute for or replace local funds, states would be in a position to restructure local school organizations. This might end the tenure of ineffective boards, those local debating societies which may do more harm than good for our students.

Relationships between these local boards and teachers' unions have become one of the stumbling blocks to advancing education. One has to wonder:

- are the school boards protecting students and the public from incompetent and avaricious teachers?

or

- are the unions the lonely and maligned defenders of efficient quality education?

I do not know of any evidence to support either hypothesis, but I know many Americans who believe they know the answers to these questions.

It is likely that local school boards and teacher organizations will be among the first to rise in opposition to the program advanced in these pages. We would hear every argument for home rule and local control conceived thus far. We are also likely to witness major resistance to any form of standardized performance. But such opposition is unwarranted.

Local schools should be operated with as much independence of centralized control as possible. Nonetheless, local operation and local control do not mean an absence of broader standards. Perhaps the outcry against such standards is an unwillingness to recognize incompetence and inferior performance.[9]

Septum Sixpack and Henna Homestead both drive their cars where they wish, when they wish, how they wish. But the various states and the federal government establish standards. Septum and Henna are limited to driving on the roadways. They must respect one-way traffic patterns. They must not drive in certain areas at certain hours. Their vehicles must conform to safety and environmental standards. And Septum and Henna themselves must meet competency tests.

So, too, we must expect and accept performance standards for our schools, students, and teachers. There is too much at stake for our nation to settle for less because we fear coordinated national efforts. Our task is to choose a path for education that will enhance our capabilities to generate income and sustain, if not improve, the quality of life we have come to expect.

"The public schools are a failure," Sheldon
explained, "and we should have the choice of
sending our children to private schools with the
taxes we pay for the public schools."

Eight

The Choices
Ahead

Merely corroborative detail, intended to give artistic
verisimilitude to an otherwise bald and unconvincing narrative.
—William S. Gilbert

We have many choices with regard to education. They have been with us and will continue into the foreseeable future. Should we continue to fund and operate our schools as we have, or should we make significant changes? Several persons of widely varying philosophies are putting forth arguments to institute such changes.

Many citizens believe that public schools are not doing the job they should and that our national economic performance is inadequate for the needs of an aging society. Some would then counsel a reduction in expectations. Others hold that a nation's economy is directly related to its education system, and call for urgent repair of that system.

Operating in this environment are political theorists who have declared war on local schools in pursuit of their philosophical aims. They employ two weapons: one is "choice," a program to treat education like other services in the private marketplace, but with the benefit of a government subsidy. The second is the flattering assumption that parents are informed consumers who seek the best education for their children. In reality, however, it may be a misallocation of resources within our education systems that needs correcting rather than the systems themselves.

The role of choice in society

The issue of "choice" helps us summarize several points made earlier in this book. "Choice" is a word that has been corrupted in our times by political movements. None of us favors coercive action, so when we can identify "the good" with "choice," we leave the opposition supporting tyranny.

The leading advocate of choice has been Professor Milton Friedman. He has been successful in building an impressive army of followers who are on a crusade to defeat a perceived entrenched enemy flying the colors of the National Education Association.[1]

Choice requires options, but they may be expensive. An ice cream shop may be able to offer 100 different flavors, but only if the cost of those variations is minimal and the demand for them warrants that inventory. So, too, a community may be able to offer a wide diversity in housing, education, and other services, if the effective market demand is present.

What if consumers at a given ice cream shop do not support even five different flavors? Perhaps there are too few consumers, or their incomes are too low for them to spend much on ice cream, or they do not have much of a taste for ice cream. We would think it silly for the government to step in. But this is just what we do with education. We do not consider education the moral equivalent of ice cream. We believe that citizens should have certain basic services

. . . even if they cannot afford those services;

. . . even if there are not enough of them to make it "efficient";

. . . and even if they do not chose to have those services.

This was the accepted belief of our nation about education and the system which provides education to our children. That consensus is now under attack and has been damaged.

If education were left to parents alone

Parents may want a "good" education for their children, but that "good" education may not be "adequate." As consumers, we need to acquire information in order to use our resources wisely. How much do parents spend of their time or money to acquire information about the education of their children? From the discouraging news about collapsing parent-teacher organizations such as PTA and PTO, from the dismal attendance at school open houses, and from parental indifference to homework assignments, we can only assume that limited numbers of parents are investing their own resources in education.

If parents wanted the "best," they would be willing to make significant sacrifices. In truth, they want only the attainable, given all their other wants and the constraints of their resources. How many parents or grandparents will give up their fine homes, their new cars, their cable TV, or their pension rights in order to educate their children or grandchildren?

If the parents do not place a high value on education, they may underinvest (from society's point of view) in the education of their children. Because society is concerned that parents will not devote sufficient resources to their children's education, we have instituted mandatory attendance laws and provided substantial subsidies for education in America.

Choice in education

What choice is there in education? One way of improving the education of children is to send them away to schools offering distinguished programs. This has been a standard practice among the wealthy for generations. Less wealthy persons have exercised choice by moving to a school district or parish which offered programs consistent with their desires as parents.

This defines the essential relationship between education, transportation, and the community. If education is not in the home, it involves transportation. And that brings us to the central choice parents make, within the limitations of income: they choose a place to live. That decision, for more than one hundred years, has linked education and residence as a package.

If you do not mind being separated from the child, and can afford it, you can send your child hundreds or thousands of miles away, and she can come home infrequently. If you are of more modest means, you will have your child walk to the nearest school daily.

Now, the community becomes important. If your child is to walk to school, then you must choose a residence that offers what you want (and can afford) in combination with a school that offers what you want (and can afford). Choosing a home and choosing a school is a combined decision for most people with children. The attributes of a home include those on the site (bedrooms, baths, view) and those of the community (quality of neighbors, stores, schools). Just as a home comes with certain operating costs (garden, heating, maintenance), it also has certain transportation costs (travel to work, stores, schools).

The quality of schools in an area depends on what people want from education, their ability to pay for what they want, and the costs of providing that education. If the schools are supported by parents alone, then the programs are determined by their preferences and their resources. But if the community (in the form of the state or the church) contributes as well, then the ideas, desires, and funds of a wider group come into play. Hence, the community (geographic or religious) has a bearing on education as long as parents accept financial support for their children's schooling. And even if all schools were private, the community would probably not allow schooling to take place without regulation.

Government and our schools

The private sector could provide education because we are not dealing with a "pure public good," that is, a service from which consumers cannot be excluded. If you cannot exclude would-be consumers, you cannot get people to pay for the service. We can easily keep would-be students out of class and, thus, education can be provided by the private sector quite readily. In addition, education does not appear to have significant economies of scale which would suggest the formation of education monopolies from which society must be protected. Hence, public provision and regulation of education services must be founded in some other principle of public interest.

It is widely accepted that schooling has a bearing on the economic and social behavior of the individual. But the benefits of primary and secondary education do not accrue to the student and her family alone. Universal literacy and basic common sets of knowledge create a more efficient society. Each individual's education is enhanced by the productive capabilities of those with whom he or she comes in contact. The educated person imposes fewer costs on society and contributes to the well-being of the community via non-market mechanisms. Hence, the schooling of an individual is not a purely private matter, but affects others in the community.

Ice cream, by contrast, is a private good. The kind of ice cream you eat has such little influence on my life that we can both treat your choice of flavors as a event of interest to you alone. There are no externalities in the consumption of ice cream. But there are externalities to schooling, particularly at the primary and secondary levels.

Government is engaged in financing education because we believe that parents, particularly, but not exclusively, poor parents, left to their own resources, would not consume (or produce) as much education as we believe is beneficial to their children and our society. However, we could have government subsidies of a purely private education system. This is the solution offered by some advocates of the voucher system.

Governments provide education services for historical reasons. When

"I think it's time to send Serina to a private school," Sheldon announced without warning one evening, when visiting with Septum.

"You would," Septum growled softly, paying as little attention to his son-in-law as custom would allow.

"Well, why not?" Sheldon continued. "The public schools are a failure, and we should have the choice of sending our children to private schools with the taxes we pay for the public schools."

"Trolley cars," Septum said, his gaze directed across the street in search of some sign of activity. "You killed the trolley cars and public transportation by not using them. You got government subsidies for homes beyond the trolley lines and then said the public system was inadequate, so we had to build more roads to subsidize your private automobile. Now, you're about to do the same to schools. Don't put resources into efficient common services and complain. Just complain about them and whine for subsidies for your 'freedom of choice.' Go ahead, kill off the trolleys again."

"Suzannah," Sheldon called. "Let's get going. Your Dad's off his trolley again."

much of America was rural and transportation costs were relatively high, schools were organized to minimize travel. Thus, we have a geographic basis to our school corporations. As neighbors got together to form school corporations, they wanted to ensure that all beneficiaries (all citizens) would participate in funding education. Hence, school corporations were recognized by legislatures and given governmental powers to levy taxes.

Diverse private schools were not feasible in areas with small enrollments where only one school could be justified. In addition, we are a nation that distrusts both government and private sector activity. It was believed that accountability would be greatest if the school management was subject to popular recall by the neighbors through the ballot box.

The current drive for "choice" in schooling is a mutation of that healthy skepticism about government. But the campaign to separate public funding from government provision of education services has a virulence that makes improvements in existing public programs difficult, if not impossible. Few people want to fix something that they are told is irretrievably broken.

If education were a private good similar to ice cream cones, no one would object to privatization. Poorer children have fewer cones of lesser quality ice cream, while wealthier children enjoy deluxe treats to the limits determined by their parents. The same would work for schooling. But the education of all children is a matter of legitimate and considerable concern to society. Hence, education for the poorest child is as important as, or perhaps more important than, the education of the wealthiest. This follows from the belief that the gains to society of educating poor children may well exceed the gains of educating affluent ones. The totality of a person is a consequence of the endowment of nature and the endowment of environment, plus the additions made in the early years of life through education. When the endowment of environment (home and neighborhood life) is deficient, the additions of education may be of greatest value to the person and to society.

"Government is a rotten solution to private inadequacies," Septum told me. I had to agree. "But does that suggest we should have inadequate private institutions in preference to any government program?" I asked.

"No," he grumbled, "but we don't have to like it."

If a voucher system is put in place, parents would be free to choose the schools their children attend. What will assure us that there will not be a deterioration in the quality of education? After all, parents may well opt for schools that provide less homework to challenge their knowledge, that offer extended hours of child care, but little instruction, and that demand unquestioned acceptance of parental and social authority. Well behaved but ignorant children may be the preference of parents.

We presume government will continue to license and regulate schools. But a free market ideologue would argue that such regulation is unnecessary. Parents, as consumers, that argument says, will quickly assess whether a school meets their educational expectations. Those schools which do not win consumer approval will quickly disappear.

This drive to reduce the government's role in the provision of education and the regulation of its content requires a determined effort to discount society's stake in education. Thus, we hear more today of the private benefits of education (income earned) than of the public concerns about an educated populace. There is an effort to advance the idea that schooling is for vocational training, rather than for developing children with the values of civilization and the capacity for expanding human capabilities.

A misallocation of resources

The modern public education system is overused by society to address non-education problems. In addition, distrust of local administrations has given us a proliferation of strangling regulations and stultifying standardization. This trend has denied schools their flexibility and their capacity to meet local and changing circumstances.

America, in its drive to improve itself, has turned to the schools as the instrument of that improvement. Racial inequities were to be solved by integrating the schools. Dietary deficiencies were to be corrected by school nutrition programs. Juvenile delinquency was to be ended by school-based programs. Flab is to be fought and culture nursed by the same system that is charged with teaching chemistry and language.

In some future time it will be written: And Americans so loved their schools that they sacrificed them to rid the world of sin and evil.

The time has come for improvement, but not necessarily the dismemberment of the public schools sought by the pirates of privatization. Rather, we should seek to reduce impediments to the successful operation of the system already in place.

Schools are very much like other organizations in society. We have seen some of our giant corporations lose their adaptability to changes in their environment. Some of our schools' inflexibilities have been imposed by added state and federal regulations. This rigidness often results from the distrust we have of our governments and our demand for their accountability. What we don't realize is that we end up imposing significant costs on our schools.

Some of the problems in schools are due to hostile labor-management relations, in which unions and administrations have become petrified partners in a destructive dance. But, as in the private sector, much of the problem may be the result of a very ordinary reluctance to change and, with too much pride, to admit deficiencies.

The current system of schooling is not, however, irretrievably lost and in need of wholesale replacement. The first order of business is to determine what schools are to do. Next, they should be liberated to do that job, and finally, teachers and administrators should be rewarded appropriately for their performance. This will probably require extricating our schools from those lines of business in which they do not have a comparative advantage.

Let's start with the basic idea set out earlier in the chapter: If education is not in the home, it involves transportation. In many regions of this country, housing developers could advertise: Buy this remote rural home. It may be way out in the country, but the taxpayers of this county and state guarantee the transportation of your child to school. Why do we do this? Why can the wealthiest citizens move to suburban estates and have their children bussed to school at the expense of retirees on fixed incomes?

Parents have a choice in residential location and should bear the full costs of their choice. They should not pass along that cost to others through the school corporation's power to tax citizens. This means ending "free" (tax-subsidized) school transportation services. Some parents will find the transportation charge a burden. For those who are poor or have special transportation problems, we can provide vouchers similar to food stamps. (If you want to privatize school transportation, do so! What educator has a comparative advantage as a school bus schedule maker?)

Some parents will continue to choose remote locations because they are willing (and able) to bear that cost. Others will choose residential locations that allow their children to walk to school. Parents will demand sidewalks and crossing guards for the safety of their children. And none of this will happen instantly. But, perhaps, it will lead to smaller schools which serve more compact areas.[2]

Smaller schools, with a community focus, have been out of fashion for a generation or more. We have had waves of school consolidations because we believed that there were significant education options and economies at larger schools. That may have been true with the technology of the 1950s and earlier, but it may no longer be valid. We have done little to change our methods of teaching since the introduction of the textbook. We have failed to employ with vigor the options which computers, video tapes and disks, as well as live interactive television, offer educators and students.

The effectiveness of schooling could be increased by reallocating the tax money now spent on transporting students and using it to bring the modern world to education. We could use those funds to make our classrooms and teachers more productive by giving them superior complementary educational resources. We could help break down the school walls by freeing education from the tyranny of place and allowing students to learn at home or elsewhere if that works for them. I believe I learned certain subjects better from the textbooks I carried home each evening and back to school the next day than I did from in-class presentations by the teachers. Other topics, for me, however, required the explanation and encouragement of the teacher. Today, through television, students could learn at home, if we made more materials available to them for that purpose. Homework the whole family could watch might be more interesting than some of the current game shows in reruns.

In addition, in today's age of distance education, we can have classes made up of students in different locations, all being instructed by a teacher of superior quality through interactive TV. Schools that are too small for specialized courses can offer diversity (choice) through electronic media. We do not use these options widely today because they are costly and because many teachers and students have not developed the skills to teach or learn in this manner. But education can be transported without transporting children.

Let's not stop with transportation. Look about the school and ask, Why is this supported by the education budget? Note I did not say, Why is this in the school? That is a different legitimate question.

Competitive sports, marching bands, drama clubs. Are we again asking the schools to do jobs that are the rightful responsibility of other organizations? Each of these are worthwhile activities, but why are they supported with tax funds? Does music instruction require a marching band complete with uniforms and an extensive schedule of competitions? Often parents will pay for these "extras" begrudgingly. They would like to see tax funding for these programs, but it is inappropriate to make such efforts part of the public's responsibility.

There is no question that young people should engage in physical activities and learn the skills of play and cooperation which sports involve. But could these efforts be financed through voluntary organizations, rather than the compulsory use of tax funds? If parents and neighbors believe in the values of rooting for old Hopped-Up High at the Friday football game, could the local Rotary Club or Chamber of Commerce provide that support?

Again, funds now used for such purposes, including the capital funds for the stadium and the Olympic swimming pool, could be released for enhancing educational productivity. It seems time to withdraw the schools from their role as

"I don't mind paying for educating my neighbor's child," Septum told Suzannah, "but I do object to buying the kid lunch, getting him to and from school, giving him swimming lessons, and teaching him to play computer games."

"Father," Suzannah responded, controlling her exasperation, "those things are done in or by schools because each one makes sense. You just want schools to be what they were when you were young. Times change."

"Could be," he admitted, "but I'm still against it."

multipurpose social service organizations and return them to their role as teaching institutions. Before we attempt to remake the education system of the nation, we might try letting the one we have do its job.

At the same time, we have excluded adults from our schools thus far. If we are to make significant gains in productivity, adults must have access to education. This does not require them to attend classes in buildings constructed for children. We can take the school's resources to the factory, the community center, or the home. Teachers can leave the buildings, or their instruction can be transmitted electronically.

Where are we going?

Vouchers, competition, and privatization will not resolve our problems if we still do not have agreement on what we wish an education system to produce. Adults are more capable of describing the desired features of a home or an ice cream cone than of the education their children should receive. We tend to view education as a means of enriching our angelic offspring while civilizing the neighbors' little devils. We also want our children to learn their place in the history and culture of our diverse world while simultaneously being prepared for gainful employment by age 17.

Presumably, government regulation of schools will continue even if we go to full privatization. But will we know what outputs to monitor, or will we just measure inputs as we have in the past? The contemporary fury over choice and control is hindering us from rediscovering education's appropriate mission and renewing our national will to support that mission.

If the claims of the elderly on the income of society are to be met, American businesses must be more profitable and American workers must be more productive. We have proposed some changes in education finance, organization, and practices. Many others are on the table. The time has come to make wise choices and move ahead.

"Honestly," Suzannah exclaimed, "I don't know where you get some of the things you say."

Conclusion

And we are here as on a darkling plain
Swept with confused alarms of struggle and flight,
Where ignorant armies clash by night.
— Matthew Arnold

In brief, this book has argued that

- America is a nation with a rapidly growing older population. These older citizens have significant claims on the income generated by workers. To meet these claims, without sacrificing the living standards of those at work, it is necessary to increase the income-generating capabilities of the workforce and the profitabilities of businesses.

- This is a national concern, not a local or state matter. Federal programs in support of older Americans (social security, medicare, and medicaid) are based on national taxes. Pension plans and individual retirement programs are heavily based on stock ownership. When people retire, they expect payouts from those stocks — dividends which result from the efforts of workers all across the nation.

- The widespread, national nature of retirement income, plus the tendency of Americans to move across state lines, suggests federal financing, standards, and perhaps governance of education programs. Education, however, is not a constitutional responsibility of the federal government, and now is not the time to amend the Constitution. Our needs tomorrow are of such magnitude that we cannot delay restructuring education while we engage in a constitutional debate.

- But we could amend our thinking about education in America. Now may be the time to reevaluate the economic linkages between generations and to establish a new concept of community, based on financial and social interdependence, rather than geo-political artifacts from the past.

- Education systems need to address the undereducated workers of our nation. Yes, we need to educate the young in our schools, but of perhaps greater importance is the need to go out from the schools to the factories, shops, and offices of our land to educate the parents of those children, adults 25 to 45 who have at least 20 years of service in the labor force ahead of them.

- To finance this effort, we should recognize the intergenerational transfers inherent in our society. Adults, through their labor, support the elderly and save for their own future. Those savings, in the form of social security taxes, should be directed toward increasing the productivity of the young (and undereducated adults).

- Federal financing of our education systems can be directed through a commission or agency based on representation from the state education agencies, just as the Federal Reserve System is based on the banking industry and insulated (not isolated) from politics. This financing should seek to provide minimum standards of performance by our schools and education programs. It should not dictate inputs or methods; it should assure each student access to necessary resources, independent of the accidents of birth and parental choice.

- Local control of schools is less than our national mythology would have us believe. The states are charged with responsibility for education because children are a collective resource of the nation, too valuable to be put at risk or abused by the whims of parental consumer sovereignty.

- To finance our immediate education needs and to provide for the retirement income of our aging population, strong steps are needed. Among the possibilities available are federal taxes on recreation, entertainment (including gambling), clothing, jewelry, food eaten away from home, and incomes beyond the current social security limitations.

Much of the foregoing will seem like a nightmare of overbearing centralized government to those who are trapped in philosophical warfare. Critics will object to higher taxes. They will decry "social engineering," or will apply some other pejorative term. But governments exist precisely to interfere with the unfettered marketplace and to provide bounds for individual behavior. Governments must act when institutions and individual actions are contrary to the interests of people organized as a nation.

Some will argue that our current systems are sufficient. Yet, many recognize that our education systems have not provided our citizens with the skills requisite for today, let alone tomorrow. Those systems have been battered by conflicting demands and have lost their focus. The improvement of education, however, may best be found in the restructuring of those systems, rather than in their abandonment.

At the same time, many worry that our retirement systems, including both social security and private pensions funds, are either inherently defective or potentially troubled. But few would deny that around the corner, just a few years into the next century, lies a set of income distribution problems for this nation. I believe these can be averted only if we raise productivity and our national income.

This book has offered a partial set of remedies that can be applied to those problems. I have left the critical questions of education reform—those affecting content, process, quality, and such—to those more qualified in such matters. But if the ideas suggested here are rejected on ideological grounds alone, let the critics respond with alternatives that meet our emerging national needs. The past has not given us the present for which we wished. Reforms that attempt to resurrect a time that never existed can only fail. The problems of pensions, productivity, and public education will not go away because we do not wish to address them.

———

The rain had driven Serina to the porch of her grandfather's house. More accurately, Serina had been driving her parents to distraction before Sheldon had insisted that Suzannah drive Serina over to Septum's house. "I've work to do, and there's too much noise here for me to concentrate," the accountant had complained.

Now, the young girl was trying to endure a dreary day by playing on the deep porch of her grandfather's house. "There's nothing to do," the child sulked, discarding the books and ignoring the coloring materials Septum had provided. "You could watch TV," Septum said from his rocker. "I don't want her watching TV," Suzannah responded. "Sit down and read one of those books, or make a picture," she told Serina. "Children need other children to play with," Septum told his daughter, trying to look through the rain at the house across the street.

"Father," Suzannah protested, "you always told me that I should learn to be self-reliant. When I wanted to go out and be with other kids, you made me stay in the house and find something to do on my own. You said it built character to be alone." "Funny," he mused, "how memory seems to go as time passes. I don't know, however, if it's your memory or mine that's deficient in this case."

"You never wanted me to play with the other kids on our block," Suzannah said, regressing to an adolescent whine. "You always said the boys were just bums, and all the girls were tramps. You never approved of any of my friends." "Probably not," Septum replied, as he tried to discern movement beyond the curtains in the Homestead house across the street.

"What can I do?" Serina complained, her voice imitating the plaintive tone of her mother. The rain seemed to be inducing a minor epidemic of self-pity. Both adults ignored her.

"Other people are important," Septum said. "Oh, now really, Father," Suzannah mocked him, "you've always said we could do very well without half the people in this town." "Never did," he said. "And if I did, I changed my mind. Seems to me more and more we need other people to help us, if we expect to be happy and secure. Can't do hardly anything by ourselves.

"Take my darling here," Septum said and indicated the little girl who had fallen asleep, her head resting on a quilted cushion. "She needs playmates and not the kind of bums and tramps you always had hanging around."

"See!" Suzannah cried, but was ignored. "If Serina is to have the right kind of playmates," he continued, "we have to be concerned about how other children are raised, what they learn in school, how they behave. And it's more complicated today than it was a few years back when you were her age.

"Today, with all this Internet stuff and the mile-high anthill . . ." "World-Wide Web," Suzannah interjected. "Whatever," he continued. " More than ever, folks must be thinking about what other folks are doing. Serina can get on a computer in school,

or at the public library, or even that computer Sheldon has at home, and she's able to chat with kids everywhere. What kids are learning and doing in Oregon and New Hampshire means something to every one of us. Both for today and tomorrow."

"Honestly," his daughter exclaimed. "I don't know where you get some of the things you say. All that beer and those cigars must be rotting your brains."

"Now, now, young lady," a mellow voice reproached gently. "Pickling and smoking have been used for centuries as preservatives to prevent putrefaction."

"Henna!" Suzannah welcomed, as Septum stuttered. "Just came over to sit a while." The widowed landlady from across the street rested her umbrella against the house. "You were so tied up in your argument, you must not have seen me coming in this rain."

"Just talk," Septum murmured, as he moved a high-backed rocker into place for her.

"Yes, Father is about to bear witness. You know he has converted, don't you?" Suzannah teased. "Converted to what?" Henna asked Septum.

"Tomfoolery . . . the girl's talking nonsense." Septum tried to regain his composure. "I was saying that Serina here needs playmates, and that means we have to be concerned about the upbringing and education of other people's children, who may not even live in this town, because of the computer and all that."

"Mrs. Homestead," Suzannah pronounced, smiling in triumph, "you have just heard the first article of faith from a born-again liberal." "Not so," Septum bellowed. "Father!" Suzannah's rebuttal and rebuke were all in that one word.

"Just because I see that we are linked to each other, dependent on each other, it does not make me a deviant, a liberal." Septum seemed genuinely offended by the suggestion. "I'm trying," he continued, "to understand the world I have to live in. And that world is filled with interconnections of strangers. Every penny of my pension, I now understand, comes from strangers. Everything I buy in the store is produced by strangers. We don't know the baker who gives us our daily bread. We don't know the folks who sell us all sorts of clothes or whatever through the mail. Some of them may live nearby, but most of them are far away, even in other countries. But what I have, and what I will have in the future, depends on others. We are at the mercy of strangers."

"Very dramatic, Father," Suzannah mocked him.

"Say what you will." Septum was now in drive mode and not to be deterred by derision. "Serina needs other children to play with. And all of us need other people just to live. I need people to produce electricity so I can watch TV, and I need folks to make TV sets and produce TV programs that I want to watch. How well others can do their jobs—can give me what I want—depends on what they know and what kind of people they are. I don't see that as being liberal or conservative. It's just plain reality."

"But, Father . . ." Suzannah was interrupted by Serina, now awake, who resumed her prior complaint, "What am I going to do?" "Do you have some chalk, Serina?" Henna Homestead asked. "Somewhere," the still sleepy child replied, but quickly managed to find a large piece among the coloring materials.

"Then I want you to take your chalk and go to the far end of the porch. That's good, right to the railing. Now look all the way down the porch to the railing on the opposite side . . . Very good." Henna had the child's complete attention. "Now take your chalk and draw the most perfect straight line between where you are and those rails at the opposite end of the porch. That's right, come on down toward me . . . very straight . . . stay in line . . . good . . . yes . . . keep going, that looks very good. Excellent, Serina!"

"I did it!" The child was pleased with her accomplishment, particularly since it had secured the attention of all three adults. "Wonderful," Henna said. "Now I want you to put one foot on that line. And now the other foot in front of that. Good, and now walk forward, but your feet must stay on that line, or you have to go back to the beginning and start all over again."

"Like this?" Serina asked, as she edged forward. "Yes," her mother replied. But with the next step, Serina lost her balance. "That's OK, " Henna encouraged, " just start over. You'll get it right, and then we'll learn some more balancing things." She turned to Septum and explained, "I did a bit of circus work many years ago. It helped me learn how to avoid falling to either the left or the right when the object is to get somewhere."

"Oh, I can't do this," Serina wailed, as she stepped off the line about one-tenth of the way down the porch. "Yes, you can, honey," Henna comforted her. "Try to think of where you are going. Look ahead. Think about the other side of the porch as your goal, a nice place to be. Don't hurry. Make sure of where you are before you take the next step." "I like this," Serina said as she made her way carefully to the one-third mark.

"Maybe," Henna said to Serina, but looking at Septum, "we could set up a tightrope for you in the backyard sometime, and I could teach you how to walk on it." "Sure," Septum was eager, "we could do that."

"It might be fun for all of us," Henna said. "You're right, Septum, people do depend on others, but we must be capable of walking alone over whatever chasm lies ahead. It's a most useful skill—learning how to stay balanced, focused on where you are going." Henna smiled at him. "I found it very helpful in reaching the security of tomorrow."

"I could get some coffee and maybe some cookies," Suzannah said, heading for the front door. She had recognized the convenience of an exit from the scene. None of the three noticed her departure.

Sources of Figures

Except in the cases indicated, the data in the figures were computed by the author from information provided by the agencies shown, and are not directly available in publications of those agencies.

1.1 U.S. Bureau of Economic Analysis

1.2 U.S. Bureau of Economic Analysis

1.3 U.S. Bureau of the Census

1.4 U.S. Bureau of Economic Analysis

1.5 author

2.1 U.S. Bureau of the Census

2.2 U.S. Bureau of the Census

2.3 U.S. Bureau of the Census

2.4 U.S. Bureau of the Census

2.5 U.S. Bureau of the Census

2.6 U.S. Bureau of the Census

4.1 author

5.1 U.S. National Center for Education Statistics

5.2 U.S. National Center for Education Statistics

5.3 U.S. National Center for Education Statistics

5.4 U.S. National Center for Education Statistics

5.5 U.S. National Center for Education Statistics

5.6 author

6.1 author

6.2 recommendations based on author's calculations using numbers provided by the U.S. Bureau of Economic Analysis and the Social Security Administration

6.3 U.S. Bureau of Labor Statistics

6.4 U.S. Bureau of Labor Statistics

7.1 U.S. National Center for Education Statistics

7.2 U.S. Bureau of the Census

7.3 U.S. Bureau of the Census

7.4 U.S. Bureau of the Census

7.5 U.S. Bureau of the Census

Notes

Introduction

1. This portion of the Introduction is an adaptation of the article "Restructuring Education Finance: A Dialogue across the Street from the Garden of Eden," *TECHNOS: Quarterly for Education and Technology*, Vol.5 No.3 (fall 1996): 21-23.

1. Perspectives on Education

1. These data are not adjusted for price increases. They are computed from the U.S. Bureau of the Census, *Statistical Abstract of the United States, 1995* (Washington, 1995), 304, 452, and 458.

2. The Aging of America and the Demand for Education

Substantial portions of this chapter have appeared previously as "Who Will Warm Your Bones?" *TECHNOS: Quarterly for Education and Technology*, Vol. 5 No.1 (spring 1996): 14-19.

1. I exclude involuntary immigrants brought to colonial America as slaves from Africa. They did not choose to leave their families. In captivity, they had only restricted opportunities to maintain intergenerational relationships. After the Civil War, their migration from the farms to the cities was in keeping with the dominant culture of the times.

2. In 1992, 63% of the beneficiaries of old-age assistance were 65 or older. Also included in social security are payments to younger people who are either disabled or survivors of persons covered by this program. To simplify, these payments to the non-elderly are ignored in the text.

3. Medicaid also provides payments to non-elderly low-income persons. In 1992, payments on behalf of the elderly accounted for 31.8% of all medicaid outlays. The same year, 88% of medicare outlays were for persons 65 and older.

4. Pension plans include stocks of foreign firms as well as those of domestic enterprises. Many U.S. companies have extensive operations overseas and income from these activities. Thus, American retirees have claims against the incomes of foreign workers. It is probably unacceptable to think that Americans would finance their retirement years through ownership of claims on the incomes of people in other lands. This might be viewed as an advanced form of capitalistic colonialism, and would not be readily accepted abroad.

3. Education and the Economy

1. "One experiment worth trying would be to offer a $500 bonus for any child who enters the first grade reading at a fourth-grade level. . . . [a] reward system that can have real impact in poor neighborhoods and change the reading patterns of entire communities." Newt Gingrich with David Drake and Marianne Gingrich, *Window of Opportunity, A Blueprint for the Future* (New York: Tom Doherty and Associates, 1984), 167.

2. Mark Rosenzweig, "When Investing in Education Matters and When It Does Not," *Challenge*, Vol. 39 No. 2 (March–April 1996): 22.

3. Ibid., 23.

4. John H. Bishop, "Is the Test Score Decline Responsible for the Productivity Growth Decline?" *American Economic Review*, Vol. 79 No. 1 (March 1989): 178-194.

5. Ibid., 179.

6. Ibid., 193.

7. Martin Weale, " Externalities from Education," *Recent Developments in the Economics of Education* (Brookfield, VT: E. Elgar, 1994), 136.

8. U.S. Bureau of the Census, *Statistical Abstract of the United States*, 1995 (Washington, 1995), 158.

9. Ibid., 58. The portion with children actually attending public schools is still less because many households only have children under school age, but we may presume their interest in the schools, nonetheless.

4. Alternative Organizations of Education

1. Friedrich A. Hayek, cited in Raaj K. Sah, "Fallibility in Human Organizations and Political Systems," *Journal of Economic Perspectives*, Vol.5 No. 2 (spring 1991): 69.

2. Robert J. Haveman and Barbara L. Wolfe, "Schooling and Economic Well-Being: The Role of Non-Market Effects," *Journal of Human Resources*, Vol. XIX No. 3 (summer 1984): 377-407.

3. Ibid., 136.

4. Cited in Lawrence A. Cremin, *American Education: The Colonial Experience, 1607-1783* (New York: Harper and Row, 1970), 181-182.

5. Lawrence A. Cremin, *American Education: The National Experience, 1783-1876* (New York: Harper and Row, 1980), 265.

6. Ibid., 265.

7. Michael B. Katz, *Reconstructing American Education* (Cambridge: Harvard University Press, 1987), 19.

8. Ibid., 43.

9. Ibid., 55.

10. Ibid., 55-56.

11. Ibid., 51.

5. How Do We Pay for Education?

1. Employment is stated in full-time equivalency. Source for these various numbers: *Digest of Education Statistics,* 1995 (Washington: National Center for Education Statistics), 5-6, 11, 44, 108.

2. Ibid., 158-159.

3. Ibid., 152.

4. *School Finance: Trends in U.S. Education Spending* (Washington: U.S. General Accounting Office, September 1995), 42.

5. Local sources include tuition, fees, gifts, and other non-governmental contributions. Nationally, they account for less than 3% of the total.

6. Unitary school districts are also found in American Samoa, Guam, Northern Amrianas, Puerto Rico, and the Virgin Islands.

7. Eric Hanushek et al., *Making Schools Work* (Washington: The Brookings Institution, 1994), 25.

8. Mary L. Fulton, "Courts Play Bigger Role in Finance," *State Education Leader,* Vol. 13 No. 2 (fall 1994): 12.

9. Alex Medler, *State-Level K-12 Education Reform Activities* (Denver: Education Commission of the States, June 1994), 22.

10. Thomas B. Parrish, Christine S. Matsumoto, and William J. Fowler Jr., *Disparities in Public School District Spending, 1989-1990* (Washington: National Center for Education Statistics, February 1995), xxiii.

11. Abstract provided in Mary Fulton and David Long, *School Finance Litigation: A Historical Summary* (Denver: Education Commission of the States, April 1993), 19.

12. Medler, *Education Reform,* 52.

13. *The National Education Goals Report, Building a Nation of Learners, 1994* (Washington: U.S. Government Printing Office, 1994), 41.

6. Who Should Pay?

1. For a full discussion of both the ability-to-pay and benefit approaches to taxation, see Richard A. Musgrave, *The Theory of Public Finance* (New York: McGraw-Hill, 1959), 61-115.

2. *Digest of Education Statistics, 1995* (Washington: U.S. Department of Education, 1995), 153.

3. The full OASDI-HI (Old Age Survivors Disability Insurance and Health Insurance) rate was 15.3%, but I have excluded the disability and health insurance portions from these calculations.

4. Data are from the National Income and Product Account published by the U.S. Bureau of Economic Analysis in the *Survey of Current Business.* The amount of funds raised would depend on the elasticity of demand for recreation goods and services. If the quantity demanded is very responsive to changes in price, we

could expect a decline in total spending and a consequent decrease in tax collections. A 10% tax, after the initial response, would not be expected to have any significant long-term effects on the broad category of recreation spending. (Some goods and services might be highly responsive because there are close substitutes that are not classified as recreation.) Rising incomes would likely offset the price effect in a short period of time. But that is a subject for another tome.

5. The same caveats about the elasticity of demand to changes in the price paid by consumers apply here.

6. Again, this is assuming that there is no significant decrease in spending associated with a tax increase.

7. Households with incomes under $5,000 are not shown in these graphs. Such households may include students and others whose spending is dependent on transfers (money from Mom and Dad) not reported as income. Spending by such households on entertainment, food away from home, and apparel and services, together, exceed the gross income of these units.

7. Who Should Run the Schools?

1. Leeper v. State, 53 S.W. 962 at 966, 968 as cited in *Encyclopedia of Education*, 1971, Vol. 8: 414-5.

2. Fogg v. Board of Education, 82 A. 173 at 175, cited in ibid., 415.

3. Scown v. Czarnecki, 106 N.E. 276 at 279-280 cited in ibid., 415.

4. An ordinance for the Government of the Territory of the United States, north-west of the River Ohio, done in Congress by the United States, July 13, 1787. *Northwest Ordinance: Essays on its Formulation, Provisions, and Legacy* (E. Lansing: Michigan State University Press, 1989), 125.

5. These two states have relatively young populations. In median age of population, Texas ranked 3rd in the nation at 30.8 years, and California was 8th at 31.5 years, in 1990; the national median age that year was 32.9 years.

6. In 1995, a high official at the Ministry of Education in Thailand told me of plans by Japanese corporations to build high schools in Bangkok. These would be high-quality residential schools where young people would be taught the skills necessary to become effective employees in modern Japanese-owned factories operating in Thailand.

7. In reality, the number is higher since the census only counted persons according to where they were at two points during that period. Many persons may have moved in and then out again, but were not counted as part of a given county since they were not resident there in either 1985 or 1990.

8. Many economists, however, still contend that the Federal Reserve has only been lucky recently and that its discretionary powers should be very limited.

9. Similar arguments are made with more authority in Eric Hanushek et al., *Making Schools Work* (Washington: The Brookings Institution, 1994), 140-141.

8. The Choices Ahead

A substantial portion of this chapter appeared in *TECHNOS: Quarterly for Education and Technology*, Vol 2 No.1 (spring 1993), 16-19.

1. For a review of current choice concepts and programs, see Mardell Raney's interview with Professor Friedman in *TECHNOS: Quarterly for Education and Technology*, Vol. 5. No. 1 (spring 1996), 4-11.

2. Critics will suggest that this is a means of eliminating transportation for racial integration of the schools. That integration, however, was mainly an attempt to bring about desirable change without addressing other factors which we did not have the courage to approach. We would not face discrimination in the housing market or in the workplace so we put the burden on our schools and our children. After a generation, we have little evidence that this approach has been successful. School integration would not be necessary, if housing markets were not segregated. But that is a condition we have not been able to remedy. Is it still appropriate to ask the schools to do the job?

About the Illustrator

Dave Coverly, the illustrator of this book, is also the author of "Speed Bump," a cartoon panel distributed to over 200 newspapers worldwide by Creators Syndicate. In past lives, he has been the editorial cartoonist for the *Herald Times* in Bloomington, Indiana, and an art director for a public relations firm. He now resides in Ann Arbor, Michigan, with his wife Chris, daughter Alayna, and personal trainer Cuppa Joe.

DATE DUE

APR 2 7 1999			

DEMCO 38-297